WALTER'S WELCOME

WALTER'S WELCOME

*The Intimate Story of a
German-Jewish Family's Flight from
the Nazis to Peru*

EVA NEISSER ECHENBERG
with
Judy Sklar Rasminsky

Skyhorse Publishing

Skyhorse Publishing books may be purchased in bulk at special discounts for sales promotion, corporate gifts, fund-raising, or educational purposes. Special editions can also be created to specifications. For details, contact the Special Sales Department, Skyhorse Publishing, 307 West 36th Street, 11th Floor, New York, NY 10018 or info@skyhorsepublishing.com.

Skyhorse® and Skyhorse Publishing® are registered trademarks of Skyhorse Publishing, Inc.®, a Delaware corporation.

Visit our website at www.skyhorsepublishing.com.

10 9 8 7 6 5 4 3 2 1

Library of Congress Cataloging-in-Publication Data is available on file.

Cover design by Rain Saukas
Cover photo credit: Neisser family

Print ISBN: 978-1-5107-2476-1
Ebook ISBN: 978-1-5107-2477-8
Printed in China

CONTENTS

Memories are the key not to the past, but to the future.

—Corrie Ten Boom

Neisser

Eduard
b. 1866 Katscher
d. 1925 Beuthen

➕

Martha Nothmann
b. 1873 Beuthen
d. 1956 Lima

Klaere
b. 1894 Keltsch
d. 1941 Lima
m. **Friedrich Freund**
b. 1888 Beuthen
d. 1949 Lima

Ruth
b. 1915 Beuthen
d. 1991 Vancouver

Fritz
b. 1895 Keltsch
KIA 1916 WWI

Walter
b. 1897 Keltsch
d. 1960 Lima
m. **Erna (Grosse Erna) Lustig**
b. 1898 Gleiwitz
d. 1972 Lima

Alberto Eduardo (Tito)
b. 1932 Lima
d. 2007 Lima

Juan Rodolfo (Rudy)
b. 1933 Lima

Helen Hanna
b. 1934 Lima

Erich
b. 1899 Gleiwitz
d. 1970 Lima
m. **Gertrude (Trude) Neubauer**
b. 1907 Karlsbad, CZ
d. 1991 Montreal

Eva
b. 1942 Lima

Kaethe
b. 1903 Gleiwitz
d. 1989 Bogota
m. **Wilhelm Simenauer**
b. 1907 Zabrze
d. 1977 Lima

Ursula
b. 1936 Beuthen
d. 2012 Bogota

Vera
b. 1939 Lima
d. 2010 Bogota

Rosa
b. 1908 Gleiwitz
d. 1908 Gleiwitz

Erna (Kleine Erna)
b. 1909 Hindenburg O/S
d. 1974 Lima
m. **Heinz Liebermann**
b. 1908 Hamborn
d. 1992 Lima

Miguel (Michael)
b. 1942 Lima
d. 2011 Toronto

Nothmann

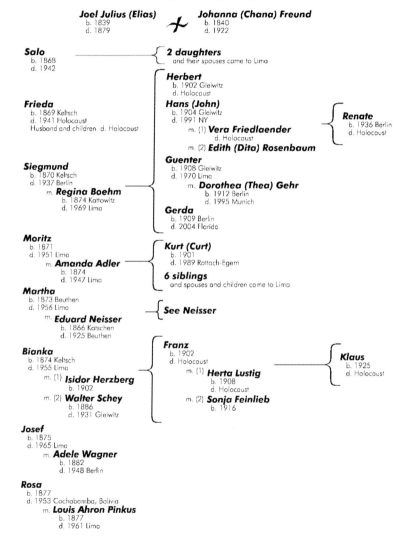

Joel Julius (Elias)
b. 1839
d. 1879

✝

Johanna (Chana) Freund
b. 1840
d. 1922

Salo
b. 1868
d. 1942

2 daughters
and their spouses came to Lima

Frieda
b. 1869 Keltsch
d. 1941 Holocaust
Husband and children d. Holocaust

Herbert
b. 1902 Gleiwitz
d. Holocaust

Hans (John)
b. 1904 Gleiwitz
d. 1991 NY
m. (1) **Vera Friedlaender**
d. Holocaust
m. (2) **Edith (Dita) Rosenbaum**

Renate
b. 1936 Berlin
d. Holocaust

Guenter
b. 1908 Gleiwitz
d. 1970 Lima
m. **Dorothea (Thea) Gehr**
b. 1912 Berlin
d. 1995 Munich

Siegmund
b. 1870 Keltsch
d. 1937 Berlin
m. **Regina Boehm**
b. 1874 Kattowitz
d. 1969 Lima

Gerda
b. 1909 Berlin
d. 2004 Florida

Moritz
b. 1871
d. 1951 Lima
m. **Amanda Adler**
b. 1874
d. 1947 Lima

Kurt (Curt)
b. 1901
d. 1989 Rottach-Egern

6 siblings
and spouses and children came to Lima

Martha
b. 1873 Beuthen
d. 1956 Lima
m. **Eduard Neisser**
b. 1866 Katschen
d. 1925 Beuthen

See Neisser

Bianka
b. 1874 Keltsch
d. 1955 Lima
m. (1) **Isidor Herzberg**
b. 1902
m. (2) **Walter Schey**
b. 1886
d. 1931 Gleiwitz

Franz
b. 1902
d. Holocaust
m. (1) **Herta Lustig**
b. 1908
d. Holocaust
m. (2) **Sonja Feinlieb**
b. 1916

Klaus
b. 1925
d. Holocaust

Josef
b. 1875
d. 1965 Lima
m. **Adele Wagner**
b. 1882
d. 1948 Berlin

Rosa
b. 1877
d. 1953 Cochabamba, Bolivia
m. **Louis Ahron Pinkus**
b. 1877
d. 1961 Lima

Walter Neisser

Introduction

ON the day my Uncle Walter died in 1960, my aunt took me to see his corpse. We walked up the stairs of the big house and down the long hall to their bedroom, where she opened the door and pushed me forward. An awkward eighteen-year-old, I had never seen a dead person before. My uncle lay on the bed, a large dishtowel wrapped around his jaw. I stared, then fled downstairs to the library where the family had gathered. Why did she want me to see him? Did she take anyone else upstairs? Was there a steady procession of mourners who came to see his corpse? The answers are most probably affirmative, for Walter was the sun of our universe, the head of the family, by far the wealthiest; he owned the business that employed most of the adults, and above all, he was the reason we were all in Lima.

Who was my uncle? Walter Neisser was a man who saved lives. He was the only one among his brothers and sisters who was tall in stature, and he was larger than life. His powers of persuasion and his deep pockets were legendary. He had lived in South America since 1923, and somehow the distance from his family in Germany and his sharp intellect allowed him to see what many German Jews did not want to admit to themselves.

Throughout the 1930s, Walter brought most of his extended family from Germany to Peru. In 1933, when the anti-Jewish laws took effect in Germany, he helped his younger brother, my father Erich, and his little sister Erna, nicknamed Kleine Erna ("Little Erna"), immigrate to Peru. Two more sisters and several cousins followed. To the entreaty of his widowed mother Martha that she could not leave Germany without her brothers and sisters, then in their sixties and seventies, Walter's answer was clear: Her siblings, their children, and their grandchildren, all members of the Nothmann family, would come, too. Of his mother's aged siblings, only one went to the death camps.

Because of Walter, some fifty members of two extended families from the German region of Upper Silesia came to Peru. Other Jews from the Silesian towns of Gleiwitz, Kattowitz, and Beuthen, where many of the Neissers and Nothmanns lived, also moved to Lima. Some came with Walter's assistance, others, like so many immigrants before them, were drawn to join their countrymen. They traveled vast distances, physically and culturally. They crossed Western Europe, traversed the Atlantic Ocean, passed through the Panama Canal and down the west coast of South America. They left behind a life and tried, in some cases successfully, in other cases less so, to start anew.

Twice, in 1935 and 1937, Walter returned to Germany to cajole reluctant family members to leave. As the Nazi laws gripped the Jewish population, he brought hope. Peru, he told them, was a place of untold potential.

But Peru did not welcome immigrants—quite the contrary. When the need was greatest, Peru passed laws to keep people out. In fact, barely 500 Jewish immigrants entered the country in the late 1930s—and Walter sponsored an astounding 10 percent of them. He had the connections, the resources, and above all the will to pay for boat tickets and procure a visa for every one of his relatives, a task that in retrospect seems almost impossible. Some family members received invitations to work at his company and therefore secured the more easily obtainable work visas, but he also arranged papers for all of the older relatives, women, and children.

Everyone lived in Miraflores, a residential suburb of Lima close to the sea, ten kilometers from downtown. Some older relatives moved in with their children; others had their own apartments or little houses, all within walking distance of each other. I have a vivid memory of my grandmother's brother, my great-uncle Moritz Nothmann, who died when I was nine and he was in his late seventies. How could a child forget him? His back had been fused into the sitting position, so when he stood, his cane in hand, his body was bent forwards at ninety degrees, his chest and head parallel to the ground. But he was not scary; in fact, he was quite wonderful. A ventriloquist and a magician, he could make coins disappear into the pockets of the suit he always wore and then reappear out of his or my ears. His other trick, one I never figured out, was to show me a coin, bang his fist on the table, and make the coin reappear below. It seemed to have gone right through the wood.

We were the only large family in the German-Jewish community in Peru, and among my friends, I was the only one who grew up surrounded by cousins, aunts and uncles, grandmothers, even great-uncles and aunts.

Walter was a prolific letter writer; he corresponded with his parents and siblings, relatives and friends. Devoted to the family, he begged for news and expressed his frustration when his letters went unanswered. One letter to his oldest sister filled two entire paragraphs with recriminations about letters sent and received.

*Moritz Nothmann, at the far left, leans forward in his chair. Beside him
sit his sister, Walter's mother Martha Nothmann Neisser, and other family
members. Lima, 1940s.*

*Our family in Lima in 1942. Walter sits cross-legged at the center-bot-
tom with the children. His mother, Martha, stands behind him holding her
youngest grandchild, Miguel / Michael Liebermann. Quite typically, my
father, Walter's younger brother Erich, is barely visible behind his mother. I
am not in the picture. Only four months older than Miguel / Michael, I
must have been taking a nap.*

Another letter contained cards with his name on them to remind family members that he would not write to them again until they had responded to his letters. When Walter received a picture of his father, who died in 1925, he wrote that the picture now hung above his bed and he would have an artist make a drawing from the photograph. His letters and his behavior make his subsequent actions much easier to understand. They show how deeply he cared for the immediate and extended family he had chosen to leave when he was twenty-six and how lonesome he was for their company. When the family's need became pressing, he was eager to help.

In a letter to his son Rudy written on January 11, 1950, Walter defined the art of letter writing:

> Your letters, in general, are extremely curt and do not correspond to my desires, nor the purpose of letters, which should be familiar conversations with an absent friend. As I want to live with my children like a close friend, and not just a father, I wish that your letters would give me a more intimate account of special events and all the events of lesser importance as well. When you write to me, think of yourself talking freely with me at home. That way you would also mention the small incidents of the day, such as where you've been, who you've spoken to, what you think of him, etc., etc. Tell me about your studies, your classmates, and the people around you. Tell me what you think of them, give your own comments, and let me see more of you.

Whereas we can read the letters one after the other, the family waited months, and in one case several years, to get news. While we note repetitions, the family would have cherished the information about health, work conditions, and birthday greetings. Letters were the only way they could communicate, and they carefully saved every letter and in many cases, every envelope.

Thanks to the members of my very large family, we have Walter's letters, pictures, and memorabilia, many letters that he received, and the correspondence of several other family members. Even though everyone moved, the letters were always packed up and shoved into yet another drawer or cupboard. I thank the entire family for not throwing them away!

Since we have letters from every decade of Walter's life except the first, we can reconstruct Walter's story through his own words and the words of those closest to him. I have opted to use the original letters as much as possible. They provide immediacy and authenticity, whereas my retelling necessarily implies choices about what to include and what to emphasize. Memory is individual, and different members of the family experienced and interpreted the same events in many ways. I was always aware that my cousins—who lived through the same period in the same place—had memories distinct from my own. Of course, when I sent them my first draft of Walter's story they were quick to seize on those differences, and I had to correct and amend the text. This final version incorporates many of their suggestions, but it clearly originates from my own particular point of view.

Had Walter's letters come to me all at once, I would certainly never have embarked on this project. At the beginning there were just fourteen, and when I counted them all at the end of this project, I had translated 113 letters and eight postcards. There are over 100 more letters that dealt with school work not done, holiday arrangements, and general discontent with Rudy that I chose not to use.

Of the letters I translated, most were in German. My German was rusty and the handwriting was often difficult to decipher, so they posed a huge challenge to transcribe and translate. Discussion among my cousins centered on the problem of translation. Should I, the self-appointed scribe, translate the letters into Spanish or English? Consensus prevailed that it should be English so that several generations of Walter's descendants around the world could understand them.

After I translated and sent out the first group of letters, I immediately received more, and it was clear that I had to put them in chronological order. The first letter we have is dated 1914, when Walter was serving as a volunteer in the German army. He was fortunate to have been wounded very early, in December 1914, and he did not return to active service for the duration of the war. Most of the correspondence we have dates from the period when he was convalescing from his foot wound.

In the 1920s, when Walter was in South America and the family was in Germany, he wrote long letters about his work, health, and friends, offering photographs and detailed descriptions of what he saw so that his family could vicariously experience his new life. Written between Walter's departure from Germany in 1923 and his first visit home in 1930, these thirty letters from Argentina, Chile, and Peru are all addressed to members of his immediate family, the majority to Kleine Erna. She thought they were so important that she brought them along when she emigrated from Germany. After Erna's death, the letters were passed down through the generations, too precious to throw out. Walter's daughter-in-law, Edith (Frankfurter) Neisser, who lives in Lima, found them at the back of a closet. When I received them, they were in a three-ring binder, organized by date. Those from Walter's first year in Argentina are in German Sütterlin script, forcing me to learn a new alphabet. Luckily when Walter moved to Chile in 1925 he started typing his correspondence at the office.

Many of the early letters are addressed to Walter's youngest sister, Kleine (Little) Erna, seen here at the far left. The beloved baby of the family, she was twelve years younger than Walter. We also have letters to his brother Erich, next to Erna, and his married sister Klaere, seated. Klaere's husband Friedrich and daughter Ruth are on the right.

There are two sets of letters from the 1930s, one from each side of the ocean. In the first set, Walter's wife, who was also named Erna—and nicknamed Grosse (Big) Erna—paints a vivid picture of the young couple's trip to South America and their first years as newlyweds in Lima. Walter sometimes adds a few words, but this is basically her correspondence. It is her letter, dated 1933, that announces the imminent arrival in Peru of Walter's siblings Erich and Kleine Erna. This section also describes the arrival of other family members, though not in letters.

The letters in the second set were written by the Lustigs, Grosse Erna's family, who remained in Germany. Addressed to Walter's recently-arrived mother-in-law and the family in Peru, they trace the unraveling and ongoing suffering of the German-Jewish world between 1937 and 1940. The last letter in this series was written in Lima and returned to the sender because the intended recipient had probably been forced to move.

During the Second World War, Walter's aunt Regina, widow of his mother's brother Siegmund, was separated from her children, some of whom were safe in the Americas, others in danger or already missing in Germany. Thanks to Regina's grandson Frank, we have their entire correspondence as well as some envelopes and photographs. Regina's letters deal with adapting to life in Lima and worrying about those in Germany. The correspondence of her son Hans, later called John, begins immediately after he was freed from Auschwitz and describes his concentration camp experience and post-camp trauma.

The postwar correspondence is sparse but varied. There are requests for money and food from Shanghai, East Germany, and West Germany that mirror the huge upheavals at the end of the war when hunger, displacement, and separation were the order of the day. These requests stand in sad contrast to the last collection of letters, most from the early fifties, that Walter wrote to his adolescent children at elite boarding schools in the United States.

It took me several years to discover that we actually had the very photographs Walter referred to in his letters, and I have inserted them in the appropriate places in the text. Walter was a passionate photographer, and all his photographs from the 1920s were brought to Lima in the 1930s. It is extraordinary that these early photos, intended for the family album in Germany, were still in the hands of family members in Peru. Other pictures came from family albums now in Canada, the United States, and Colombia.

Walter and Erna's formal wedding picture, taken on October 19, 1930, acted as a catalyst for this project. It is a visual depiction of Walter's family before the Hitler years, when they had no idea that catastrophic changes would soon force them to leave Germany. When my cousins and I started to identify those present at the wedding, we recognized many relatives. Here was this great-aunt, that uncle, that cousin, that parent. We were able to identify about half of the sixty-five people in attendance. Most of the ones we knew had come to Lima or gone to Buenos Aires. My generation, born in Peru, never met the people who stayed behind, and we were unable to identify them. We don't know what became of them.

Another incentive to write this book came from specific requests. Walter's grandchildren were searching for more information about the family, and in response his daughter Helen wrote a text that I have used as a source. More than seventy years have passed since the characters in this tale were forced to flee Germany, and the generation born in Lima is getting old. If we don't tell Walter's story now, it will be lost and those who follow will never know what happened.

Yes, this is a Holocaust story, but it is also very much the story of the importance of family and a testament to the fact that one individual can make an enormous difference. Walter Neisser was such a person. This is his story, and ours, told through the voices and images carefully saved by members of the extended Neisser, Nothmann, and Lustig families.

Note on Translations and Sources

Most of the original texts used are in German, one set is in Spanish, and there are a few letters in English. Those in German are in two scripts. The most difficult are the letters written before the 1930s in the German Sütterlin script. The letters written in the 1940s are in modern script and many are typewritten. Three letters had been transcribed and translated professionally from German to Spanish years ago, and Frank Nothmann originally translated his grandmother's letters, but I translated the rest from both German and Spanish. I take full responsibility for the content of all of the translations.

In cases where the script was indecipherable, I have used ellipses, and I have sometimes modernized punctuation in order to clarify meaning. To be consistent and avoid confusion, I have used *ae* instead of *ä* in names (*Kaethe* instead of *Käthe*). I have changed Kurt Nothmann's name to Curt in keeping with the way he spelled it while he lived in Peru. (In German it is written with a *K* and in Spanish with a *C*. When Walter refers to him in letters, he automatically used the *K*.) Another name change I have respected is that of Walter's son, Rudy, short for Rodolfo. His name was originally spelled Rudi but he changed the final *i* to a *y* to make it less Germanic. For the spelling of other names I have used the database provided by the Cementerio Israelita de Lima. For the women, I have included both the maiden and the married name, thus Walter Neisser's sister is called Erna (Neisser) Liebermann.

As I worked my way through the letters, I silently thanked my father, Erich Neisser, who was adamant about German being our home language. Like all children, I wanted to fit in, to speak the language of the country where I lived, but when I answered him in Spanish, he would pretend not to understand. German, he insisted, did not belong to the Nazis but was the language of Goethe and Heine.

The people listed in bold went to Peru.

<u>Seated on the floor in front of the bride and groom:</u>

Eva Lustig, Ernst Lustig, **Lutz Berger,** Maja (Loebinger) Gorland.

<u>Row 1, seated, from left:</u>

Bianca Lustig, unknown woman, unknown man, unknown woman, Salomon (Sally) Lustig, **Martha (Nothmann) Neisser, Erna (Lustig) Neisser, Walter Neisser, Fanny (Lanzer) Lustig**, three unknown women, Fanny (Lustig) Glaser.

<u>Row 2, standing, from left:</u>

Bertl Lustig, unknown woman, **Hennie (Nothmann) Eckert ?,** unknown woman, unknown man, **Max Lustig, Margot (Lustig) Berger**, Rudi Lustig, Maria Teresa (Maruca) Gariazzo, Wilhelm (Bill) Lustig, Gertrud (Glaser) Lustig, Angela Schymiczek, two unknown men, unknown woman, **Kaethe (Neisser) Simenauer**, two unknown women.

<u>Standing between rows 2 and 3:</u>

Three unknown women on the far left, two unknown men on the far right.

<u>Row 3, standing, from left:</u>

Herbert Nothmann, Gerda (Nothmann) Colbert, **Guenter Nothmann**, unknown man, **Friedrich Freund**, three unknown men, unknown woman, **Tilde Nothmann, Curt Nothmann,** two unknown women.

<u>Row 4, standing, from left:</u>

Three unknown men, **Erich Neisser**, three unknown men, **Klaere (Neisser) Freund**, three unknown men.

<u>Top row:</u>

Ruth (Freund) Angress, Erna (Neisser) Liebermann.

The official wedding picture of Walter Neisser and Erna Lustig, October 19, 1930, Gleiwitz, Germany. Walter's youngest sister, Kleine Erna, and her best friend and niece Ruth stand together in the very last row. Walter's brother Erich (my father) is fourth from the left in row 5; their older sister Klaere is in the same row, fourth from the right; sister Kaethe is in row 2, third from the right; and mother Martha sits in the front row, beside the bride.

Walter (center), with his older siblings, Klaere and Fritz. Gleiwitz, 1898.

CHAPTER ONE

The Best Greetings Are Sent to You from Your Loving Mother

The Neisser Family, 1897–1915

WALTER was born into a middle-class merchant family of well-established, comfortable German-Jewish shopkeepers. Although they lived in Upper Silesia, more than 400 kilometers away, they regarded Berlin as their point of reference, their capital, their cultural and economic heart. Culturally and emotionally they were Germans. They spoke German, felt German, read the German classics, enjoyed the arts. For other Germans, Upper Silesia was a backwater, but for the Neisser family it was home.

Today in modern Poland, Gleiwitz, Kattowitz, and Beuthen are considered one entity. Even when Walter was a child at the beginning of the twentieth century, the three cities in Upper Silesia were closely linked. They were all border towns where the borders kept shifting. Three uprisings ended with a 1921 plebiscite to decide where the border would be drawn. The German-speaking population chose to remain in Germany, but the League of Nations awarded Kattowitz, the biggest of the three cities, to Poland. We know for certain that the Neisser family, like the rest of the Jewish population, was German speaking and identified completely with the German faction.

When Walter was fourteen, shortly before the First World War, Gleiwitz had a population of some 61,000. Its economy was based primarily on mining, and the mines and their related industries drove many of the cities' enterprises. There were also distilleries and iron works. Gleiwitz had a very active and thriving Jewish community that included a large synagogue, a Jewish school, an old people's home, and two cemeteries, as well as all the other related institutions such as a chevra kadisha.

The Neisser family had lived in this region of Upper Silesia since at least 1790, when surnames were given to Jews in the Breslau area. (Before that date, Jews were known simply as "son of.") Following the common practice of taking place names, the Neisser family derived its name from the nearby river of the same name, sometimes remembered as the Oder-Neisse, which marked the border between Germany and Poland (1855–1916). Because the family name stems from the River Neisse, there are many Neisser families. Most are Jewish.

Jews were not allowed to hold citizenship in the European nations until the nineteenth century. Walter's great-grandfather, Simon Neisser (1755–1859), was the first in the family to become a full-fledged Prussian citizen. He received his citizenship on March 24, 1812, when Napoleon declared that Jews had the same rights as non-Jews; and because Simon lived to the age of 104, he had many years to enjoy his new status. His son Hirschel Neisser, born in 1785, was but the first of many Neissers to fight for the Fatherland. A veteran of the Freedom War against Napoleon, he was buried with military honors and the ringing of church bells. When the town pharmacist complained to the King of Prussia that church bells should not ring for a Jew, the King replied that church bells should ring for all his soldiers.

Walter's parents, Martha Nothmann and Eduard Neisser, had seven children. Klaere, the eldest, was born in 1894, and Erna, the youngest, fifteen years later. One son, Fritz, born in 1895, fought and died during the First World War; another child, Rosa, lived only seven months. If anyone had told them that all five surviving siblings and their mother would live most of their adult lives in Lima, Peru, and eventually die there, they most certainly would have laughed. What a preposterous idea! Why would a family so well established in Germany leave their home? They had lived in the area for as long as anyone could remember.

Martha and Eduard Neisser.

Although the first three children were born in Keltsch, a small village, the next four Neisser children were born in Glei-witz, where there was more opportunity for commerce. Like so many Jews, Walter's parents were shopkeepers who sold clothing. They must have prospered, for in his letters Walter uses the plural, "stores," so there were at least two. When Walter and his siblings were growing up, Gleiwitz was part of the German Empire, then in 1918, part of the German Federal Republic. Subsequently the area was divided, and the towns have been Polish since 1945. Gleiwitz became Gliwice; Beuthen became Bytom; and Kattowitz is now called Katowice. The distances between them are very small, less than thirty kilometers from Gleiwitz to Beuthen, and from the correspondence we know the Neissers lived in both towns and moved easily between them.

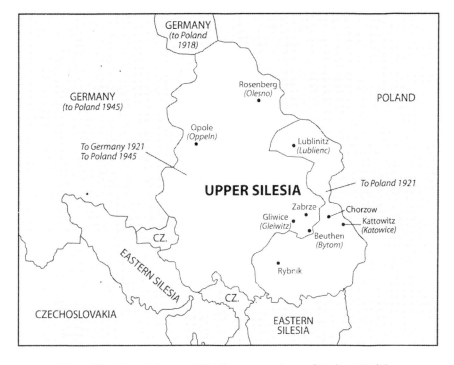

Upper Silesia is a little over 400 kilometers southeast of Berlin, 300 kilometers east of Prague, and over 800 kilometers west of Kiev.

In one of many letters to his son Rudy, Walter remembers his hometown in the following manner: "I was born in a village that had some 700 inhabitants and what you saw most were trees. What I like most today is a natural setting that resembles the place of my birth." He could not have remembered the village itself because my father, Erich, only two years younger, was born in Gleiwitz, but Walter might have remembered the general area.

Walter was a poor student, but somewhere along the way he honed not only his writing skills but also his leadership qualities. As an adolescent he ran away from home and made it all the way to Austria before being dragged back by the authorities. We know little else about his childhood except that he became a stamp collector very early. It was a lifelong passion that allowed him to dream about other countries, traveling by means of his imagination.

Walter and his siblings most probably received a formal religious education. I have inherited four of my grandmother's prayer books. Three are bilingual, German / Hebrew, and the daily prayer book is in Hebrew only. If Walter's mother Martha read and prayed in Hebrew, and my father read Hebrew, so presumably did Walter. I also have my father's tefillin, not that I ever saw him lay them for they surfaced only after his death.

Certainly the most famous relative, albeit from a different branch of the family, is Dr. Albert Neisser (1855–1916), who discovered the causative agent of gonorrhea, *Neisseria gonorrhoeae*, the bacteria named in his honor, as well as the causative agent of leprosy. Dr. Albert's father was a Jewish doctor, Dr. Moritz Neisser, but Albert Ludwig Sigesmund Neisser's name evokes the integration of German Jews into the German mainstream and the reality that if German Jews were to get ahead, it was best to convert. His decision would have been typical of the professional Jewish population of the late nineteenth century, many of whom converted in order to take up medical or academic positions. In 1882, at the age of twenty-nine, Dr. Albert was appointed professor extraordinary at the University of Breslau. Although it is likely he did not consider himself Jewish, everyone around him most probably did.

There are unmistakable parallels between Dr. Albert Neisser and his wife Toni, a well-known philanthropist, and Walter and his wife Erna. Dr. Albert and Toni built "Villa Neisser," a large home in Breslau that they filled with paintings and beautiful objects. As great patrons of the arts they hosted concerts at their home, and musicians (Gustav Mahler, Richard Strauss), writers (Gerhard Hauptmann), and many others visited their salon. Dr. Albert donated the villa to the city with the proviso it be used as a museum. His wish was granted in 1920, but the Nazis confiscated the property in 1933. Walter Neisser named his first son Albert, a clear reference to the eminent scientist. Did he also share his view that it was best to convert to get ahead? Walter did not convert but hedged his bets by educating his children partly in Roman Catholic schools. Walter and Erna built big houses; they were great patrons of the arts and had important collections of antique silver and stamps. In addition, they were renowned for their house concerts.

Walter and his two brothers served in the German army during the First World War, and from that experience we have pictures, letters, and postcards. Walter volunteered when he was seventeen, was wounded in the right foot in December 1914, convalesced for months, and was never again sent to the front. From his correspondence we know that he served and was wounded somewhere in Lorraine, in northeastern France. The town he mentions, Septsarges, is in the district of Verdun, one of the bloodiest battlefields of the war. For his service, he was awarded an Iron Cross.

Fritz, the eldest, a dental technician by training, became a war casualty. He must have been buried in a mass grave, for when his father Eduard died nine years later and their world still seemed safe, he was remembered at the bottom of his father's tombstone with the words, "In loving memory of our son Fritz who died fighting for the Fatherland on May 15, 1916." Since Eduard's wife Martha is buried in Lima, her space on the double tombstone is empty. My father, Erich, was drafted after his brother's death and surely that death influenced his behavior in the army. He suffered from bad acne and scratched until his entire back became infected. He was hospitalized and managed to stay unfit for service until the end of the war. His back was badly scarred but he claimed it was well worth staying out of battle.

Fritz Neisser, Walter's older brother.

The tombstone of Walter's father Eduard with the inscription for his son Fritz, in the Glei-witz cemetery.

The correspondence that follows allows us a tiny peek at both family and national events. There are letters not only to and from parents and siblings, but also from the close-knit extended family. We can see from their willingness to serve in the military and from their partic-ipation in civic organizations that they were well integrated into the German mainstream. Walter's first letter was written shortly before he was wounded.

From Walter Neisser to his father Eduard Neisser

5 December 1914, Cuisy

Dear Father,

I received your dear letter on the 3rd and am very happy about the same. For the two packages you sent me which have arrived, 1 with sausage and 1 with [. . . meat . . .], I send you my heartfelt thanks. Instead of sausages, please send me fat more often, since every now and then when we can go to the headquarters at Septsarges, we can buy sausages. If you send along a [. . .] you will always get a letter in return (of course it cannot be too thin, small or soft).

We have just baked and therefore don't have active duty. Yesterday the volunteer soldier Sergeant Johannes v. Anlok was buried in Nantillois, and emissaries, me among the volunteer soldiers, were sent with wreaths. There is a bigger hospital there and I met a man from our company wounded on the night patrol of the 3rd. Now it is very quiet here. The continual, incessant, reciprocal, exciting night attacks have eased up and the losses are not as great. Our shelters have been expanded, so we live in quarters that are mostly rooms. The lieutenant is well disposed toward me and I get along splendidly with my superiors. Going for walks is a little different here than at home. The terrain is tremendously difficult and we mostly train in another way. The volunteer and replacement soldiers therefore practice extra jog-trots but mostly under the lieutenant's command. For active men the slow walk [inside the trenches] and being wingman [on the far side] are very hard. I had the misfortune to get the corner, which the lieutenant thought, and then said, was funny.

When this letter goes out we will just be marching straight into the trenches.

Be cordially greeted and kissed by your loving Walter
Fritz should send me a letter immediately and you as well.

From Fritz Neisser (1895–1916) to his brother Walter (Postcard)

2 January 1915
Address. Antonienhütte in stamp / Army postal service. To the war
volunteer Walter Neisser. Reserve military hospital (orphanage)
Lichtenthal Baden-Baden

Dear Walter,

How did you spend your birthday? I have not written for a
long time but thought of you often. In [Thüringen] Thuringia, I
wanted to write to you every day; the parents just did not send me
the address. I expect my marching orders any day.

Two [groups?] must go today. It is generally thought we go to
Turkey. What is true in that, I do not know. How are you otherwise? How is your injury? About myself I have nothing more to say
other than that I'm fine and I await my call-up notice with stress.

Greetings and kisses from your brother Fritz

From Walter Nothmann (1896–1915) to his cousin Walter Neisser

20 January 1915, Neu-Ruppin
Dear Walter,

Have received your card even if there is very little in it. I will
answer your questions. In a night attack before [Loveit] I fell into a
ditch and pulled a tendon. I marched along until after [Skernilwiese].
Then I could [walk] no more. Now that's all done and I'm just here to
recover. About your wounds I am not clear. Write me exactly [what

happened]. Erwin [a cousin] was shot in the lower leg and lies in Berlin. All three of us came back from the field in one week: Erwin on December 17th, you on the 20th and I on the 23rd. Erwin and I both belong to the 5 Res. Regiment, but I did not know it. What military unit do you belong to? Write me soon and be greeted many times by

your [cousin] Walter

Postcard from Regina Nothmann to her nephew Walter. Side A.

Berlin, 25 February 1915
Welfare Card, The Fatherland Patriotic Women's Association,
Provincial association Berlin for the benefit of the war welfare

Volunteer Neisser
Hospital Resident, Orphanage
Lichtenthal Baden

Dear Walter,

We received your card and were glad that you are well; I hope you make a complete recovery. Walter Nothmann and Erwin are no longer in the hospital; for the time being they are at the Thorn garrison for 4 weeks. We are sending you some cigarettes and many greetings

from the dear uncle, the boys, and your aunt Regina

Postcard Side B. Moritz von Bissing, a Prussian general originally from Silesia, was recalled to active duty during the First World War and served as Governor-General of occupied Belgium.

From Eduard Neisser to his son Walter

24 March 1915

Dear Walter,

You are probably guided by the saying that you will be measured by the same measure that you measure others. I consider this to be false if you judge by the correspondence we send you and you complain [about]; and now, in the hospital, you have a lovely, long

Walter, at far right, with crutches.

Walter, center, weaving baskets while convalescing.

time to write home in detail. But your reports are as thin as the bread rations. I have some rheumatism now and it is my intention, if nothing intervenes, to visit you after Easter and maybe take a few [thermal] baths in Baden-Baden. Greetings from all of us, and from him who has always loved you,

your Father

[Postscript from Schimansky] Get well and hope to see you soon, [I] wish you well with many regards, Schimansky

[Postscript from Walter's mother Martha] The best greetings are sent to you from your loving mother. Why don't you sometimes write your grandmother? She's annoyed about it.

Walter was discharged in the summer of 1915 and started working in Gleiwitz in one of the many plants owned by the coal magnate Fritz von Friedlaender-Furd, a convert and one of the richest men in Germany. Presumably this was an office job, for his foot was never fully healed and he comments that he does not have to walk far. Sadly we do not know how long he stayed with the company, when he left, or why. What is clear is that he gravitated to the energy sector from his earliest years.

From Walter to his brother Fritz

18 August 1915

18.VIII Since yesterday I am employed at the coal works Company Em. [Emanuel] Friedlaender & Com. [Company], owner Fritz v. Friedl. [Friedlaender]-Furd and receive a salary of M. 100 per month, pension M. 80 [expensive _____]. I like it quite well here and I do not need to walk very far. In a short time I expect detailed letters from you, and then followed by a letter from me. Receive greetings and a kiss,

your brother Walter

c/o Frau Rosenthal Oberwallstr. 8

This is the world Walter left in 1923 to seek his fortune in South America. He is in the right foreground, arms crossed.

Walter in Germany before his departure for Argentina. Dapper and handsome, he poses for the photographer in a pin-striped suit, the inevitable cigarette between his fingers.

CHAPTER TWO

I Have a Great Deal of Work

Argentina and Chile, 1923–1927

GIVEN the terrible economic conditions in Germany, with high unemployment and rampant inflation, Walter's departure was a gamble, an immigrant's dream for a better life. Like the majority of immigrants at the time, he headed first for Buenos Aires. Argentina in general and Buenos Aires in particular were focal points for European immigration, for it was widely believed that Argentina had the same potential as the United States. Millions of immigrants arrived, the most numerous from Spain and Italy, but Poles, Russians, Germans, Greeks, and Jews also came by the hundreds of thousands. In the year 1900, immigrants made up half the population of Buenos Aires and work was easy to find. By the time Walter landed in 1923, immigrants were still pouring into the country but work was scarce. Like most immigrants, Walter arrived penniless and took whatever job came along. In his first year, he was a butcher, a butler, a farmhand, and a teacher.

From Walter to his youngest sister, Erna Neisser, aged fourteen

26 October 1923, Urdinarrain, Argentina

My dear little Erna,

Thank you very much for your dear letter. I am sorry to hear that you were sick for such a long time and I hope that you are now completely healthy again. I am well and I have to play teacher for 1 to 3 more weeks. I teach 3 boys and 2 girls reading, writing, and arithmetic. I live at a farmer's who has 8 children, 4 of whom I teach; the other 4 are still under school age.

I took a picture of the family and I am sending you a sample. The corrugated iron house is the school here, much like a junk storage room where [I], a photographer of old stuff and similar junk, stay. Beside my bedframe the chickens brood and raise their little ones, and during the night animals such as fleas and the like visit me. But otherwise it's very nice. The food is excellent and I would like to send you the many eggs, cream, and all the nourishing things that we have here every day and in large quantities. Every farmer

The family Walter worked for at their farm in Urdinarrain, Argentina.

has many, many cows and horses; the farmyard is left to the geese, laying hens and chickens, four dogs, and the riding horses that live there.

There are no stables here and the homes of the people in the country are mostly made from [. . .] dung shaped into bricks or corrugated tin or tree trunks. One part of the house in the picture is made of clay [adobe], the other of sheet metal. I'll send you other pictures from here another time because now I have to ride over to the neighbors and have no time to look for more since this letter has to go to the [railway] station. Here the harvest begins in a month and it is unbearably hot in the summer, while where you are it's cold and winter. Even now it is very warm.

If you write again very soon, you'll get more pictures from me. Warm greetings from your loving brother,

Walter

[Horizontal:] Tell Erich that I am very angry with him.

Walter took this picture of a tinsmith in Argentina, "Hojalatería de Ludovico Moelinger."

From Walter to his sister Erna

18 December 1923, Galarza, Argentina

My dear little Erna,

Warm but late congratulations for your birthday and I wish you all that is good and beautiful. In this letter, I'm including 5 pesos for you and you can buy something with it or keep it without exchanging the money. Because you described the gentlemen's room so nicely for me, I want to describe what my house and I look like!

[My house is] a large furniture wagon with 2 doors and 2 built-in wooden windows, a large long box for storing food; I sleep on top of it. Then a built-in box for tools, oil and grease for the machines; bags on the floor intended for the fruit. We are just harvesting flax, which is then immediately threshed in our machine.

I run around with a wool shirt, a large black cloth around my neck so the sun does not burn [it], a long black swath around the waist so I don't overstrain and [it] also holds up my dirty blue mechanic's pants; and on my feet, white cloth shoes with straw soles, and sunglasses. The whole outfit is crowned with a wide-brimmed hat. I'll send you a picture so you can tell everyone, stay in Europe, otherwise you'll soon look like the man in the picture. Otherwise, I'm doing pretty well and the heavy work agrees with me. Write me again very soon, and for every letter you'll get 50 cents from me. I hope all continues to go well for you and warm greetings,

Walter

From Walter to his family

18 December 1923, Galarza, Argentina,
Urdinarrain Hotel Union (where Walter receives his mail)

My very dear ones!

I received your letter and was very pleased about the same. I am doing very well but now I am doing <u>very</u> hard physical labor. For 14 days I was a blacksmith and mechanic and helped repair the harvester. 12 to 14 hours of work a day and now, for the last 6 days, I've been out in the fields with the machines. From sunrise to sunset, 4 x 4 consecutive hours per day. Only when it rains do we rest. I am the assistant to the machinists and at the same time clerk. First I have to be at the machine, check it, smear it and oil it; and then, when the machine is working, I'm at the scale. There, I receive the full bags, lift them up, and remove them from the scale. Each bag [weighs] about 56 Kg. [I] lubricate [the] machine at all chow breaks and take care of tools and eating utensils.

In addition, we live like pigs. With 12 local [men] and 2 [. . .] horses [. . .] (my bosses also have a large mill) we work out in the fields in extreme heat. The heat alone is already unbearable, add to that the hard work, and at night, when you fall over like a log, you are tormented by the bugs; it is indescribable. The mosquitoes, fleas, and the worst plague of all, the tropical insect "Bicho Colorado." When you are not used to this, you sleep poorly. Even now, as I write, I have to scratch myself constantly. The only advantage is that I live in the sleep wagon. Just like over there [in Germany] it's a furniture carriage for tools and the boss has given me a mattress and my 2 blankets.

Working with the blacks is not easy and it is only good for me because I already speak pretty good Spanish. My income is very decent; <u>everything</u> free and 130 pesos per month. As a blacksmith I got 6.00 per day. However, that is worse than 130.00 a month because when it rains there is no outside work. Unfortunately the harvest lasts for only two months and then you can be on the road again. If you don't know about the wandering life yet, you can learn it here. I met a man from Upper Silesia here who has been in Argentina for 14 years and is always on the move. 3 men from Upper Silesia met by chance in Urdin. A weird rarity. Am sending along a picture of it [the encounter]. I look like a black man.

Walter, center, with two men from Upper Silesia.

I'll also send you some pictures in front of the machine because I look like the locals. To give you an idea of how we live, I'm sending Erich a picture of my boss [at the place] where I taught school.

The farmers build the houses in such a way [that] they can move them. [Their houses are built] out of dung from the street and straw, or out of corrugated tin. A European cannot picture how people live here and it is difficult to describe in only a few words. One thing is certain: Every German worker has a better-built house and lives in greater comfort than most locals who live in the country-side in Argentina. In the countryside, one can earn only during harvest time. This is short and not enough for the year. If it works, I'll try to be a machinist next year. That means there is no way here to make plans [for the future] because even the harvest is like a lottery ticket with 1000 possibilities for failure. Rain, hail, frost, and locusts are the most important factors. Today we worked only ¼ day; it rained and the rain comes down differently here than where you are. That's why I'm able to write so much.

I have to finish for today. I have to stand while I write and my legs already hurt. Please send cordial greetings to Friedrich, Klaere, and Ruthel and all others and I apologize that I cannot write everyone individually.

Cordial greetings from your loving brother,

Walter

From Walter to his family

21 March 1924, San Andres de Giles, Argentina

My dear ones,

Today I will give you only the latest news because now my time is very limited. As I told you, I recently worked in a German slaughterhouse but nothing came of it because the two companies could not agree. I went on to Buenos Aires where the situation was extraordinarily bad and [I] had long waits and found no job. For this reason I took a job at an estancia, a large landholding some three hours outside Buenos Aires. There I work as a man-servant, a plate juggler. I have already broken the largest of their serving plates and today broke the cover of the sugar dish. Luckily nobody has said anything. They are local people; [they] have two married daughters and one unmarried. Besides Spanish, they all speak English and French. An English "miss," 1 English nanny, a Spanish nanny (for the 4 children of the married daughter who live here in the summer), a cook, a maid, 1 chauffeur, 6 male servants, and my poor self care for only the boss during the winter (the womenfolk spend winter in their house in the city), and in summer, we care for 9 people. I have my own house to care for. It has dining and billiard rooms, guest rooms, larder, breakfast room, children's dining room, and my storage place [pantry]. That is where the dishes are and I prepare everything. We rise at 6. Breakfast is at 6.45. Then [I] have to tidy the dining room, then have 1–2 hours for my own ablutions (bath, etc.), then set the table for lunch. That takes at least ¾ of an hour, same for the evening, just to prepare the big table for 6 people. I toast the bread, [place the] wine, liquor, water, butter, cheese, fruit, etc. I must ready and then serve. The first day I made many mistakes but now it goes splendidly. Today all have left in the car (a Benz Wagen) and I have some letters to write. I am all right, but have taken this job only in order to be close to Buenos Aires where I can soon find a job in a commercial business. My friend Daner is going back on the *Cap Polonia* on the 27th. If my chances don't soon improve, I will do the same or go to North America or find a wife. Whatever comes up! (Dr. Contelly sews bags in a meat refrigeration business.) One warns the curious about Argentina.

My health is very good. Since everything is well again, all is hunky-dory. My salary is $55 with no expenses. I hope all of you are well and with best wishes,

your Walter

Address: W.N. Buenos Aires Moreno 740

———

A chance meeting with one man changed Walter's fortune and transformed both his professional and his sentimental life by finding him a good job and a good wife. Thanks to Rudolf Lustig, Walter started working in Chile for Ferrostaal, a subsidiary of AEG, then a binational Dutch-German company, now a huge multinational. The conglomerate also included OSRAM Licht AG, today a multinational lighting manufacturer headquartered in Munich. AEG built power stations and sold steel, rail cars, and material for the mining industry. Ferrostaal has had sales offices in South America since the 1920s.

Clearly Rudolf Lustig saw Walter's potential and the two men first became friends and then relatives. They were both Jews from Upper Silesia, Lustig from Gleiwitz, while Walter's family was living in Beuthen. Certainly the fact that Walter was good looking, good natured, and already fluently bilingual was a big help. Ferrostaal was Walter's introduction to the world of light and power and he stayed in that industry for the rest of his life.

———————

From Walter to his sister Erna

14 October 1924, Santiago, Chile /
Letterhead: Richter and Cia. Sucesores de Aug. Samhaber /
Santiago, Calera, Valparaiso, Santiago

My dear little Erna,

It has been a long time since I received news from Europe. In the meantime I have moved to another country and completed a wonderful journey over the Cordillera de los Andes, the largest mountain range in the Americas. The journey crosses at an altitude of almost 4,000 meters across mountains that are more than 6,000 meters high. I could still see things from the previous Indian inhabitants and could photograph the ancient bridge of the Incas. I already have a very large number of photographs. Now on my trips to the south, I will have ample opportunity to get acquainted with the most beautiful parts of the Americas and again take innumerable photographs. Soon I will make prints of all the images and send you one of each. I fear that you won't be able to keep them for very long.

Walter's photograph of a river crossing the jagged Andes mountains.

At any rate, I am quite well again and a few days ago I went out to a lavish lunch with Mr. Lustig from Gleiwitz and Händler from Beuthen, paid for by Lustig in honor of my arrival. There I met Mr. Händler. Listen to this. He asked if I was active in the leather industry and if I was a professional butcher. Of course, in great astonishment, I asked why, and he told me that he had been asked by a gentleman in Beuthen if he had met me in America. In addition, he was shown a letter of mine from northern Argentina where I said that I was currently working as a butcher.

Here in Chile, which is not even remotely as large as Argentina, they don't know the conditions that prevail in the neighboring country and [the Chileans] are very surprised when they hear about everything you have to go through there [in Argentina] and almost always ask you first: Why didn't you come straight here? The trip from Buenos Aires to Santiago de Chile costs the same as one to Germany. To get the fare together you have to save for quite a long time if you have such a poorly paid job.

Here in America, all social change is very rapid. A month ago, I was still a servant, and now I am a member of the German Club that is the most distinguished German club here. I am delighted to take part in it.

How are things in Germany and how is the Mischpoche? How are you dear Ernele, and how is school? How are the stores? I would be very happy to have news from home soon and hear that you are all still alive and well. Write soon and sincerely greet all from your brother who loves you.

Walter

From Walter to his sister Erna

[No date. October or November 1924 or 1925]
My dear little Erna!

I thank you very much for your kind letter but I was not pleased with your report card. It is not good; we hope that the next one will be better. If you do well in 4 subjects, I'll send you a nice gift. An Indian handicraft. It is a big animal hide with an Indian head drawn and burned into it. So make sure that I can send it to you soon.

Meanwhile, warm greetings, Your Walter

From Walter to his mother Martha (Nothmann) Neisser

2 January 1925 (*sic* 1924), Santiago, Chile,
Letterhead: AEG Compañía Sudamericana de Electricidad
My dear mother!

For your upcoming birthday I send you my heartfelt congratulations and everything good and beautiful, but most of all I wish you good health and I hope that you will celebrate the day and spend it quite cheerfully and happily surrounded by the entire Mischpoche.

I am sorry that after such a long absence, I cannot join you again, but I believe that sooner or later it will be the case, and that I will then find all of you, although a few years older, in the best of health.

Thank God I am well physically and in business, although I believe in this letter I will again report a disappointment. In your last letter you ask why I say nothing about my work; however, the reason

Rudy Lustig and his wife Maruca.

for that is I was fired a few days after my arrival. Although they have not given me a real reason, it is generally supposed that the notary of this so-called friend does not work with Jews.

Since the dismissal took place before the contract was signed, I had to accept it without having received the reimbursement for the trip, almost as much as from Europe to Buenos Aires. Because dismissals are only allowed in 4-week periods, he had to keep me in his office for two months in order not to harm his prestige as a businessman too much.

On the recommendation of Lustig, who became engaged to a local woman at Christmas, and with whom I get along very well, I got a job in the accounting [department] at AEG. So I have been lucky again and have not made a bad exchange because as you probably know, AEG is one of the best-known companies in the electrical industry and has an outstanding reputation and of course is a better springboard than Richter and Cia. I am getting a starting salary of 350.00, and on December 31st, they already paid me 220 pesos for the first half-month, a sign they are pleased. Moreover, I really learned how to work in Argentina and you will be [surprised] to know that your son Walter is, on most days, the first one in the office and you don't have to think this is an exaggeration; it is a fact that today I arrived at the office at 6 instead of at 9.30. Yes, previously I did not believe I could do this but it is coming along and it is going well. Moreover, you do not have to believe that this is only at the beginning. Oh no, here you will be shown no mercy like where you are; those who cannot make it are left behind and I want to go forwards, soon and forcefully. Moreover, the recommendation of Lustig, who is highly regarded here, makes it a duty for me to be hard working, and he told me that he has proposed me as the administrator for the German hospital in May when the present administrator is going back to Europe.

So when, dear mother, you will have this letter in hand, you'll note that despite all the zigzag [. . .] I have quickly made progress and that even [though] it was sometimes very hard, I have worked my way through it quickly. For example, many don't believe that I have spoken Spanish for only 1½ years. And when I consider that I actually never really worked in an office, it is a great deal that here, in 8 days, I was able to get used to working in an unpleasant and not easy job which took my predecessor 4 weeks, although he knew nothing except accounting.

In a few minutes it will be midnight and the day that begins my 29th year will start, so an age where you have to wake up before it is too late, and I want to make the most of the two years before [I'm] 30. So dear mother, when this letter arrives it will have been 4 weeks since I raised a glass to your health and you can do the same.

Again good luck and quite affectionate greetings from your loving son,

Walter

━━━━━━━━

In the 1920s Walter was still very unsure where he would finally settle. He often mentions that if a specific situation does not improve, he will move on to either Buenos Aires or North America. His decision to stay in the Americas is firm, and despite the hardship he first met, he is eloquent in his enthusiasm about the New World. Only once in the entire correspondence does he voice the possibility of going back to Germany.

He spent almost three years in Antofagasta, Chile, as a salesman on commission for AEG. At the time Antofagasta was the world's biggest saltpeter (sodium nitrate) mining area, the mainstay of the Chilean economy and Chile's second largest port. Then saltpeter was used in fertilizers and gunpowder; today it is used in rocket propellants and fireworks. Forty years before Walter's years in the region, the War of the Pacific (1879–1883) was fought over the ownership of the saltpeter mines. Chile defeated Peru and Bolivia and took possession of the Atacama Desert, which it holds to this day.

━━━━━━━━

From Walter to his sister Erna

23 May 1925, Antofagasta

Muy señorita mía or My dear little Erna

. . . I've settled in here pretty well, also have a large number of acquaintances, am a member of the Tennis Club and the German Club and played tennis for 2 hours today. Last Sunday I played tennis from 8 to 10 ½ [10:30] in the morning then went on a small outing on horseback with my predecessor Klaus Hollaender, son of the famous Felix Hollaender who I hear is from Leobschutz and (also) an accountant. They gave me a racehorse because the other horses had all been allotted and I said I did not care which one I got. We mounted and rode on the street. I had a small racing saddle, and I weigh only 63 kilos, so for the horse it was a godsend because although [he was] described as tame, he was quite the contrary and immediately galloped. The saddle, which was strapped quite loosely, slipped and I almost fell on my nose. I got off, tightened the saddle, and got back on again. I probably tightened the saddle a little too firmly, because the minute I mounted, the animal started to prance and broke into a racecourse gallop. My companions galloped after me, but in a few moments they lost sight of me. My horse wanted to throw me off and I couldn't control him. An idiotic soldier blocked the only avenue in the middle of the road, jumping around like a wild man, thinking he could stop the horse this way. Of course he achieved the opposite. The horse gets by, jumps up on the sidewalk and puts the children at risk. I pull him down, make a quick turn to bring him to a halt, and we both end up on the smooth asphalt. I hurt my left arm a bit, then swapped the horse for a tamer one and we rode around for a few hours. When I got home I could barely move the arm, had the arm massaged a few days and today I was back on the tennis court. So it ended happily and next Sunday I will take another horse right away. Otherwise unfortunately there is nothing else going on here.

Antofagasta is the second biggest port in Chile and the capital of the province of the same name. It is about as big, 187,000 sq km, as the whole Rhineland and Bavaria and has only about 100,000 inhabitants. Of this total, the city has 78,000 and the rest live elsewhere in the province. There is nothing but a nitric desert and nothing grows; there are no trees, no shrubs and nothing green. There are no animals, no birds; they can be found only in the area where the workers live. Fleas are also imported. It's a huge wasteland and called "pampa" or "desert." In German it is "desert." Even the vast Cordillera here is completely without any greenery and has a sad, almost deathlike appearance. We rode around in it, and there is absolutely nothing, absolutely nothing but stones and sand. From time to time one finds shells, a sign that earlier it was covered by

A photo of Chile that Walter sent to his family.

the sea because the distance to the sea is extremely small. Beyond are the high mountains. Life here is just like the landscape. No vegetation. There is only a small avenue planted with trees, which cost an enormous amount, because the water for this purpose, even the drinking water, is brought down from the high mountains from a distance of about <u>300 kilometers</u>. Here there is no rain whatsoever; it comes only once in several decades and then it rains for only a very short time, maybe 1 hour. It is the region with the least rain in the world and therefore the richest in saltpeter. There are no cafes, no restaurants, at best those like in the Graupenstrasse, and for the better public, clubs, expensive, boring and bad. In a word, I don't like the city at all.

People here party a huge amount and I am currently not interested in that; the city possesses only two large beer breweries. I will spend my time practicing sport and especially working. Work is interesting but spending all my time at the office is also not satisfactory. My three predecessors lasted one year, 10 [months], and 9 months respectively, and I do not know if I can stand it any longer. In any case, I don't think so. If I am offered a well-paid post in Germany while I am here (about 1,000 gold marks), I will possibly go back for some time. Well, until then, there are still a few days' time. Otherwise there is nothing world shattering to report here. I personally am healthy, alive and well, except my arm hurts a little bit; [I] hope you will soon report the same. Write me in detail and surely you'll get news more often and in more detail since I am in the office on Sundays and Fridays and there are a huge number of holidays here.

So warm greetings to all but especially to you from your [. . .]
brother, Walter

Because of the angle, with the sand in the foreground and Walter at the far right, it is clear he took this photograph with a timer and ran to sit down, cigarette dangling. Note his car in the background.

From Walter to his family

28 August 1926

. . . Business here is extraordinarily quiet at the moment and I have to work very hard to sell and earn sufficiently to cover all the expenses. Until now (touch wood), I have been able to manage this and I'm happy if it does not get worse. I think that when the crisis is over, we will be able to earn well here and then I will surely be able to set aside a few marks for my European trip.

Currently I am avidly training for the tennis championship next week and have signed up for both the singles and doubles matches. My chances are quite poor but maybe I'll be in the top 10 or 20 or possibly even in the first ten. Three months ago I was between 40th and 50th, so this would be a very acceptable jump. I hope the large audience will be quiet, so I can be the same. Otherwise, there is nothing new to report. I hope to have news from you again soon and send warmest greetings to all,

Walter

Walter, in profile, holds the racket like a guitar at the sports club in Antofagasta.

From Walter to his family

31 May 1927, Antofagasta, Chile

Letterhead: Walter Neisser

My very dear ones:

In the last little while, I have been blasted [by work] and so much has happened that I really need to apologize that once again you have had to wait such a long time for news. I had just started a business letter (in the typewriter), and when suddenly Lustig's letter fell into my hands, I took it out to write you a few quick lines. I received your letters and such, and indeed a detailed letter from Lustig. I wanted to answer in the last few days, but it just did not happen.

Above all, I thank you sincerely for the news and I am glad that everyone is alive and well. I also wanted to give my special thanks to [the] Friedrichs [his sister Klaere, brother-in-law Friedrich, and niece Ruth] for the reception you gave Lustig and wife. He described your wellbeing to me in great detail, [told me] about life in Beuthen and about the food; he did not even forget to mention the wine he drank with you. Mother was especially sweet and nice and supposedly looks like a thirty-year-old and like Klaere's sister.

Walter's mother Martha and his sister Klaere in Germany.

He described everyone [in the family] and also mentioned that Erich was a great help to our dear mother and that [the store] was the best place for him. Mrs. Maruca liked Erna very much and she writes particularly about her. I would have liked to have been there and sincerely hope that it might suddenly be possible for me to slide over there for a short visit to see what's going on.

As for myself, my health is good and so is business, except the business here is dying. As Lustig told you, we have been experiencing a crisis for a number of years that is getting worse instead of better. German artificial saltpeter now competes with natural Chilean saltpeter and the decline in sales of the Chilean product has been going on for more than a year. The vast majority of local companies that produce saltpeter have enormous stock and have therefore ceased operating. Work was expected to resume on 1 June because on that date the prices fixed by the Trustees cease. However, tomorrow is already 1 June and there is no talk of a work resumption.

Walter's photo of the Antofagasta saltpeter operations.

Almost every country in South America has one principal product, and the prosperity and the [financial] movement of the entire country depend on it. Brazil has its coffee, Argentina grains and farm products, Bolivia tin, and Chile has saltpeter. The saltpeter industry is dead and of course the entire business life of the country has been acutely affected. Antofagasta is the center of the entire saltpeter industry and because of the work stoppage has been hit the hardest.

Our business deals mostly with new plants or extensions of electrical systems. These are power stations and companies that need large amounts of electrical power, therefore the purchases they make are for large sums. Only secondarily, or rather in emergency situations, [do we deal] with retail sales and storage. Because of the aforementioned closures, our business has now become nothing but a junk shop. We have huge stocks, and not only have to pay for these but on the contrary incur losses. My predecessor had stockpiled an enormous technical inventory that has not moved for two years and eats up vast quantities of interest that we have to pay to our factories.

Two months ago, as I believe I wrote you, the chief of all Chile branches was here. He suggested I should stay here for at least two more years since work is expected to resume in June. These prospects did not materialize, however, and 8 days ago three directors—a big shot from Berlin, the supervisor for all of South America from Buenos Aires, and the uncle from Santiago de Chile—came to see the sick child.

Walter, far left, and Rudy Lustig, third from left, with important AEG visitors from Berlin and Buenos Aires. Walter refers to his mentor, Rudy Lustig, as "the uncle from Santiago."

The situation of the northern Chile branch was discussed in detail. The unfortunate heirloom that I have to manage was declared terminally ill and no longer viable. It will be restructured and revert to what it was years ago, an engineering office with a technician who has some samples available, and his sales will be handled from the factory in Berlin. I am to unload the huge inventory in three months, wind up the office, dismiss all employees. Every man is going overboard; I have been given a relatively difficult and unpleasant task. I don't get any instructions and I am responsible for everything and manage as best I can. They sweet-talked me, saying that the only consolation was that they hoped they had given such a difficult task into the right hands. In recognition for my work, I am the only one who will be transferred to another branch and I have proposed Buenos Aires. However, I will wait to see what conditions they propose and possibly find better prospects in Santiago and a position with a different company.

You understand that under these circumstances I cannot complain about lack of work since I have already made three car trips through the saltpeter desert and only returned again last night from Tocopilla. I took one drive before the gentlemen came (they were only here two days) in order to be able to report accurately about the situation at the different operations, which meant I sat in the car for 4 days with few interruptions. In any case, you should not think that this is a pleasure because here there is nothing that can be described as a road. Through the pampa one drives almost exclusively in old tracks and gets shaken up. I will have to get rid of the car I recently bought for business trips and also dissolve my nicely furnished house. However, these are collateral results of a wandering life, which over time, one has to become accustomed to and cannot be taken too seriously.

If I go to Buenos Aires and my budget allows it, I'll try to get a short European vacation so there is a possibility that I'll visit you at the end of this year. Don't get your hopes up a lot because things turn out differently than one thinks.

In any case, write soon to Antofagasta so the mail reaches me here. After the first of August, please send the mail to Rodolfo Lustig, Santiago, Calle Nueva York (calle means street), with whom I'll get in touch as soon as he arrives. So all the best and cordial greetings to all.

[Cursive:] Am enclosing a quick picture

[. . .] Your loving Walter

CHAPTER THREE

Miraflores Is Like a Summer Resort

Lima, 1927–1933

IN November 1927, AEG transferred Walter and Rudy Lustig to Lima. With Rudy as the boss and Walter as his second-in-command, they worked at Ferrostaal, a subsidiary of the German multinational.

From Walter to his family

> 4 November 1927
> RMS *Essequibo*

My dear ones!

Since the day before yesterday I, along with Lustig and wife, are aboard the *Essequibo*. We have just left Antofagasta. Tomorrow morning we arrive in Iquique; then come the ports of Arica, Mollendo, and at last, Callao. From there we have a ¾-hour drive to Lima.

We arrive in Lima on the 9th and I start working immediately. I will probably stay in a hotel in Lima the first month and then take a room in a suburb by the sea since it is apparently very hot in the city center. I will most likely again buy a car in order to live far from the office, which always pays because these homes are significantly cheaper and this also usually has a lot of benefits.

It's 11:40 at night. The lights of Antofagasta are still visible, and once again I steer full steam ahead into a new future.

If this means a final good-bye to Chile, I do not know. In any case, it closes one of the most important stages of my career. I hope for the best for the future and I hope for continuing good health.

I hope to hear from you again soon that all are healthy and cheerful and that business continues to do well.

Warm greetings to all of you from your Walter

Photo of Lima sent to the family in Germany.

Peru, and specifically Lima, was very different from Argentina and Chile—and a world away from the German town Walter had left only four years earlier. Peru was not a desired destination for immigrants. Unstable politically, the country was dominated by a land-holding class that had no interest in business. The powerful Catholic Church adamantly opposed freedom of religion; sanitary conditions were poor; illiteracy was high; but above all, it was the lack of business opportunities that kept newcomers away. The majority of immigrants were Chinese and Japanese men brought into the country to work as coolie laborers in jobs as disparate as the building of railroads and farming on cotton plantations. The few Jews were small businessmen.

Walter was no doubt welcomed by the tiny Jewish merchant society in Lima. Yet his letters reveal a secular businessman. He provides only a few clues that he is Jewish: Instead of the word "family" he always refers to the "Mischpoche"; he jokes about kosher pork; and he makes just a passing comment about the fact that he was dismissed from his first job in Chile because of his religion.

In 1930 there were three distinct Jewish communities in Lima. The first, the Sephardic group, came mainly from Turkey. The second, the Yiddish-speaking group of Ashkenazy Jews, hailed from Eastern Europe and the Ukraine. The third, the German-speaking Ashkenazy Jews, tended to be liberal and had little interest in religious practices. The numbers were minute: The German-Jewish community totaled 400, and the other two combined a mere 1,500. All of them were recent arrivals to the country and everyone was poor. They did not

Walter newly arrived in Lima.
November 1927.

necessarily live in the capital; many owned small shops in provincial cities.

Handsome, blue-eyed, smooth-talking, multilingual, and friendly, Walter quickly made friends among the Peruvian elite. In either 1928 or 1929, he was engaged to be married to a Peruvian lady whose last name was Benavides, one of the wealthiest families in the country. This engagement did not come to fruition, but he was clearly making powerful friends. In an inspired move, he joined the Masons in January 1929 and made connections with the new business elite rather than the old landowning class. Although still an employee of Ferrostaal, Walter now moved among rich, influential Peruvians and had the ear and the support of the most important business people in the land. It was during this time—that is, almost immediately after his arrival—that Walter made one or several friendships that later were lucrative beyond his wildest hopes.

Walter's application for membership in the Masonic lodge Logia Fraternidad y Progreso Nº 28, jurisdicción de la Gran Logia del Perú, dated January 1929, is a world away from manual labor in Argentina. Walter is thirty-one years old and gives his religion as "mosaic," from Moses, meaning those who follow the faith of Moses, a term then in fashion.

From Walter to his sister Erna

17 March 1928
Letterhead R. Lustig, representante de Ferrostaal,
Lima, Casilla 1167

Dear little Erna,

I received your two letters (one arrived at the same time as Ruthel's) and I was very pleased to hear that you are always gay and cheerful.

The day before yesterday I returned from a business trip I made by car with a companion. I have a great deal to do because next week I have to travel yet again. Within the next three months, I want to visit most of the country, which, considering the local roads, is no small feat.

Now I'm going into the interior for 2–3 weeks and after that for about 2 months to the north. My last trip took 14 days and I put 1,504 kilometers on my car. About the trip itself, which was interesting but difficult, I will write later and [send] pictures.

So don't scold. Otherwise, I'm very well and I am as black as a Negro. I think in Beuthen you would deny I was your brother. Therefore I'll wait [to visit] until I am somewhat whiter.

Image of the Lima cemetery on a postcard Walter sent to Little Erna. He finishes his message on the photo.

Please excuse the handwriting and the pencil but I'm rushing.

Please greet everyone on my behalf and be greeted yourself by your brother

Walter

Hotel Huacapistana, where Walter stayed in Chachapoyas, a remote town in northern Peru.

From Walter to his sister Erna [Postcard]

1 July 1929, Ayacucho

Alemania, Srta. Erna Neisser, Beuthen U/Schles.

Reichsprasid. Platz 13

Dear little Erna,

I have been traveling for some time and am currently in one of the oldest cities of the Americas. So don't be surprised [that] you have not heard anything from me in a long time; I am preparing for my departure for over there [Germany] and then will tell you all about it personally. Lustig is in Chile until the end of July [. . .] and I will probably not leave until the end of next month. Meanwhile cordial greetings to all,

Your brother Walter

From Walter to his sister Erna

14 August 1929
Letterhead Walter Neisser

Dear little Erna,

Many thanks for your various letters which I have received and you are right when you complain bitterly about my well-known writing laziness. I won't even try to apologize since I know you don't believe me, and although I wrote you some postcards anyway, those apparently don't count . . .

Although he mentions his desire to get married only once in his correspondence, Walter is going back to Upper Silesia to get married. Rudy Lustig, who was instrumental in finding Walter his first good job, also found him a good wife. Like so many matchmaking immigrants before him, Rudy told Walter about his single cousin, Erna Lustig, who was also from Gleiwitz, and a long-distance match was arranged. We have no correspondence between Walter and Erna, but they were probably engaged before they met because in the long letter that follows, written several months prior to his trip back to Germany, Walter instructs the family that only his mother is to meet him and Erna at the train station. He probably met her for the first time in Breslau, away from the family, but this is pure speculation.

Confusion arises because of her name. Since his little sister is also called Erna, it is unclear who is meeting him in Breslau, his bride-to-be or his little sister. Yet if it were the little sister, there would be no reason to tell the family to stay away. We have to conclude that he did not want his future wife to be overwhelmed at the train station by his gawking siblings. The family would distinguish the two women by calling his sister Kleine Erna (Little Erna) and his wife Grosse Erna (Big Erna) because of the difference in their height. All the Neisser brothers and sisters were short, the sisters barely five feet, Erich five foot three when he stretched. Walter, the tallest, towered several inches above the others. Grosse Erna's family, the Lustigs, were tall, especially when compared to the Neissers.

━━━━━━━━

From Walter to his family

17 February 1930
Lima, Peru P.O. Box 1157 Letterhead Walter Neisser

My dear ones,

The financial statement has gone off to Germany, the inventory has been completed and the warehouse relocated—along with my holidays. The replacement is settling in and I finally have some time to think about myself and improve my neglected personal correspondence a little.

You will surely say those are lame excuses. Unfortunately, that is not the case, but I was really overwhelmed with work and I already looked neglected and badly groomed.

In the last few days I've caught up a little bit and in the next little while I hope to have more opportunity to make my travel arrangements. It is now finally clear that my European holiday will start in May. Therefore I have sold all my carpets and am now looking for a lovely buyer for my car. Hopefully one will soon be found so he can start making the payments because here too everything is paid in installments. No one has money—everyone wants to sell, no one wants to buy. Currently most cars that are being bought are sedans. The opportunity for business may be poor, but this is the best time to travel.

Walter's car.

Carnival, 1928.

Walter did not use the car just for work. The same señoritas appear in several pictures.

Kleine Erna wrote she had already given up waiting because [she knew] I would postpone my trip once again. But this time it is real; it's certain that I'll take the gondola [ship across the Atlantic] unless something extraordinary comes in between. But let's not assume that my new assistant, a Mr. Jacob from Cologne, who started his job well, [will] run off after such a short time. Lustig of course is also a bit selfish because I am his inseparable companion, secretary, friend, boarder and deputy. I could certainly have gone earlier but he would not let me go. Now I have said enough and he and Essen [city, headquarters of Ferrostaal] have agreed that I'll go in May and he'll leave upon my return. However, he'll go first to Chile, then to Ecuador, and then maybe in March to Germany. When I get back, he can stay away an entire year; I really don't care. I too have earned my holiday, although it is usually the case that one gets a trip to Europe at the end of a three-year contract and then only if it is expressly mentioned in the contract.

With the next post I'm already going to start sending magazines with statistics, etc., over there [to Europe] and ask you to keep them for me. I'm going to need them and the only reason I'm send-ing them now is that I fear I will forget them. My first mailing is the magazine *Ciudad y Campo*, where you'll discover my striking features on page 25.

Walter at the tourist convention in Lima as de-picted in the magazine Ciudad y Campo.

The opening of the tour-ist exhibition in Lima. Carnival, 1930.

This picture was taken at the opening of the tourist conven-tion that I had the honor and pleasure to attend. Conventions are now the order of the day, and I'll probably have the opportunity to attend the Electricians' Convention (just imagine) in Berlin.

I am in good health. Business could be better but one must take comfort because no one is lying in a bed of roses these days. My profits turned to vinegar this year because of a large bankruptcy and a lot of tax write-offs on the old warehouse, and rotten customers have swallowed up my earnings. But what can you do? I hope this year will be better and that at the end of the year 1930 a little [money] will be left over.

How does it look at your end and how is business? Has the winter business been up to what you had hoped for? And brought the expected sales up to a level so that you can welcome me with a properly roasted goose with cracklings? But kosher and if possible no cooking samples by Kaethe or [Kleine] Erna; frankly in this case I prefer mother's well-tested recipes. But you must not think that I eat badly here. On the contrary, my stand-in mother, Maruca Lustig, takes excellent care of my physical wellbeing. Currently she has a cook she can be proud of. Last week she roasted a duck that Lustig and I devoured entirely in one meal and I can still taste the delicious fat dripping from my lips. You know, it has to float in fat. The girl is naturally quite dark, but a culinary artist. Only she can't make a lemon cream and I can't leave until the same, or at least the recipe is here, so please hurry. How are you otherwise and what else is new there? What is Erich doing? Does he have a job and where? Will I be there to attend Kaethe's engagement and what should I bring as an engagement gift? Or will Ruthel, pardon me, my big niece Ruth, be engaged first?

For your information I would like to announce today the following: I don't know my itinerary yet; however, I think that I will stop first in New York City, where I will be staying a few days for business reasons, and then will to go to Essen directly. From there I go to Breslau, where I want to meet Erna [Lustig]. Together we will travel to Beuthen, and if possible, I would like only mother to pick us up at the station.

I don't have any other plans yet. But as I wrote earlier, I must have six weeks free [to be] at the disposal of the various factories. This is all in 6 months, and the entire trip is about 10 weeks long, but the ample time necessary for the factory visits cannot be altered.

For today, I'm going to call it quits and [I'll] write [my sister] Erna by the next post. I will bring plenty of pictures, and in addition, I've just bought a little movie camera so you can see Lima and I can seduce you with my life here. Meanwhile I still hope to receive several letters from you, and as I await them, I remain with sincere greetings for all.

Walter

The window of the Ferrostaal store where Walter worked when he first arrived in Lima. It features Osram lightbulbs and the sign reads "Luz es vida," light is life.

From Walter to his family

10 May 1930

Lima, Ferrostaal G.m.b,H, Essen Sucursal de Lima

Representaciones AEG, OSRAM, MAN, MIAG

My dear ones!

When you get this letter, I will already be in New York. From there, on June 19th, I will take the steamer *Hamburg* and arrive in Hamburg on June 27th and come directly to Beuthen. The departure from here was delayed, this time not by us [but] because the departure times were changed. The [people] in Essen had reserved the steamer *Santa Maria* from here to New York and the *Bremen* from New York to Hamburg. The steamer *Santa Maria* is now going to leave on the 27 of this month instead of June 3. I therefore would have no connection to the *Bremen* and am instead traveling on the *Hamburg*. Too bad. But this way I can be in New York for 7 days and take care of some business. According to the contract, I have to be available for 6 weeks at the factories. So at first I will stay in Beuthen for only a few days. Do not forget to prepare a well-roasted goose and cabbage and cake.

I hope to see you soon and have a healthy reunion,

your Walter

━━━━━━━━━

From the pictures we have, Erna's family seems more affluent than the Neissers. Nevertheless, we may be getting an incorrect impression, for at the time photographers supplied both outfits and backdrops for their clients. Erna is the older of the two girls. It is fitting that she is wearing a hat, for she loved hats and wore them often and well. We know little about her younger sister, Hilde. At age eleven she fell down the stairs and died.

Erna, aged nine or ten, with her sister Hilde (1900–1911) and their mother, Fanny Lustig.

A triptych of Erna and her parents, Fanny and Salomon Lustig. Gleiwitz.

Some of Erna's relatives were professionals, including her uncle, who was a prominent lawyer. But her father, like the Neissers, owned a fine-clothing and undergarments store. During the First World War, he served in the German army and was wounded on the Russian front. According to family gossip, that is when he contracted syphilis. He became increasingly feeble and died in 1935. Erna's mother, Fanny Lustig, did not work in the store; she kept house.

From the correspondence we know that Erna was sophisticated and cultured. She studied music, traveled to Italy, and worked in her father's store from the 1920s until her marriage and departure in 1930. She was thirty-two years old and certainly considered an old maid when she married Walter, who was thirty-three. Is that why she accepted his proposal? It is astounding that she, being an only daughter, left her parents alone in Gleiwitz. Perhaps they simply wanted to assure her marriage. Or was she swept off her feet? What could she have imagined when she saw the engagement ring, a four- or five-carat marquise diamond surrounded by twenty or more small diamonds? Today it belongs to her daughter, Helen.

Erna's letters are very different from Walter's in both subject matter and style. While his sentences are long and descriptive, her language is telegraphic, with clipped, short sentences. His letters are long, hers are short. She writes about domestic problems, friends, and later, about her children. She also writes about the weather, a subject Walter seldom mentions. She never buys writing paper, always uses Walter's office stationery, sometimes from previous years. Well after he had founded his own company she was still using the paper from his time with Ferrostaal.

It is remarkable that Erna's very first letter—and a very short one at that—reveals so much about her. She likes clothes, music, and travel.

The newlyweds shortly after their splendid wedding, as shown in the photo on page xxiii.

———

From Erna (Lustig) Neisser to her mother-in-law Martha (Nothmann) Neisser

26 October 1930, Century Hotel, Antwerp, Belgium

Dear Mother Neisser!

I want to write you and your loved ones a few lines before we leave. In Cologne, I was alone, because Walter had 1½ days of work in Essen. He rang you, but accidentally requested my parents' number.

Here it rains continuously. We want to visit the exhibition [The Exposition of 1930] in the afternoon. Then Walter has to watch *The Blue Angel. Manon* [Puccini's *Manon Lescaut*] is being shown at the opera but my things are already on board. We go there tomorrow morning at 10 o'clock. Apparently the steamer will be fully occupied. We have already picked up our tickets.

Kisses and greetings from your daughter Erna

Cordial greetings to: Freund family, Kaethe, Erna, and Walter

━━━━━━━

(I assume that her regards at the end of her letter are a mistake for she writes "Walter" instead of "Erich.")

How did Erna manage when she first arrived in Lima in 1930? Were those early years hard for her? Did she have trouble learning Spanish and adapting to a new country with different customs? At that time Lima was a true backwater, and the poverty around her must have been a huge shock. Her letters give few clues.

━━━━━━━

From Erna (Lustig) Neisser to her sister-in-law Erna (Neisser) Liebermann

14 November 1930

My dear Erna,

I, too, want to wish you the best on your [twenty-first] birthday. Above all a man just for yourself. Stay healthy and sincere greetings and kisses from

your sister-in-law Erna

From Erna (Lustig) Neisser to her sister-in-law Erna (Neisser) Liebermann

21 January 1931, Lima
Letterhead Walter Neisser Casilla 1472

My dear little sister-in-law Erna,

Today we received your dear lines from the 27.XII.30 for which we thank you many times. I hope that our dear Kaethe is well again. She should always wear woolen (satin [. . .] also) underwear. You're surprised that I can cook! Yes, what you do for your sweetheart is twice as good! But cooking is not a pleasant occupation, especially if you have a battle-ax maid who does not help you. This is already the 4th one; she has a 1¼-year-old child who after an entire morning leaves my ears ringing. Well I won't put up with this for long. Also, I have to go to the market every morning because of the great heat (82 in the sun). Nothing lasts more than one day. We don't have an ice box yet. Then I struggle with the coal stove, the soot from the chimney—spits into the kitchen. Sometimes I look—like a chimney sweep or Black Peter and Walter has to [wipe] my face so he can give me a kiss when he comes to the table.

[She resumes four days later.]

Today our newest jewel started! The 5th one [maid]. I assume that this one will work out. But I felt the same about all the previous ones!

A good remedy for chilblains: Soak the feet in hot water, as hot as possible; add one large piece nut tannic acid (drugstore). Wounds may not be present.

Today we were informed that the trunk has arrived; tomorrow it will be picked up from customs.

[Rudy and Maruca] Lustig will probably be leaving [Peru] in February or March.

I suggest that you and Kaethe go to Capri in May or September. If not there, then go to Berlin. Also not to be scorned and not so far. Angela Schymiczek and Ilse Kornblum can give you the best advice because we always traveled together. Since we are more interested in the merits of the place, we travel in the fall when there are good, cheap grapes.

And, speaking of grapes, the grape season here is right now. A kilo costs 25 leut. = 0:30 marks! The strawberry season is over! I also made jam! Right now, in summer, we have the most wonderful fruits that cannot be transported. The last thing I needed, she [the maid] wants to try everything. And everything was supposed to grow in our garden! Walter always stops me if I want cuttings.

But now I have to close! You give us great joy! For you, dear mother, Klaere, Kaethe, Erich, Friedrich and Ruth kisses and sincere greetings,

your Erna

Included 2 pictures

From Erna (Lustig) Neisser to her sister-in-law Erna (Neisser) Liebermann

6 November 1931
Letterhead OSRAM

My dear sister,

I have neglected you so much even though you are so good and write us so often. First, grateful thanks for your two letters with accounts of your travel experiences and the nice photographs of Pörschach [Austria]. I am happy that you and Kaethe spent such nice days. Walter and I are both in good health. We don't need a rest because we now live here in Miraflores, which is like a summer resort, although [we live] modestly; we hardly go to the movies, maybe once a month. We live happily, like never before (that is my case—if it is the same for Walter, he'll have to tell you!). The film *The Blue Angel* just opened here. The Europeans are delighted, of

course—the Peruvians probably less so because they cannot understand the individual characters well. Their taste tends more to the
North American kitsch with a "happy ending."

Walter poses with a parrot; Erna is busy in the background. Miraflores.

Now that my cold is finally completely gone, I am again busy
with my singing and have recently acquired a student, to whom
I teach bel canto. Mrs. Adler, wife of Engineer Adler (also [at]
Ferrostaal), wants to sing a few songs with a trained voice for her
husband's birthday in January. Certainly a nice surprise! I was just
interrupted by a visit from Libia Llosa [member of an elite Lima
family]. She was just doing her visiting rounds.

. . . [Top line of page missing] Then I think it is the wind, have
I hit the bed so hard that both the floor and door banged? There was
a strange noise on the street and I thought a strange car was driving
by! The next morning I could not get over the jolt during the night.

I kicked the foot of the bed—but the door did not move. Walter had slept well and I told him about the events of the night. Oh you were dreaming, he said. Witnesses and acquaintances confirmed what I had observed during the night. The strange noise on the street was a side effect of an earthquake. When you live on the first floor [the North American second floor], you feel the movement much more. Many people went out onto the street. We live on the ground floor and consequently felt it less. During the night I certainly did not know what was going on and slept well the rest of the night.

Recently, the men's bowling night included a ladies' event. It was quite nice. I bowled so badly that I came in next to last. Why should I do better than my husband? Please inquire how much the lowest cost would be for a second-hand baby carriage. If it is second hand, we can get it into [the country] duty-free. The Rudy Lustigs could bring it via Bachmann, Hamburg. For now, all my love to you, dear mother and the siblings,

from your Erna

[Walter adds] Kind regards Walter
Enclosed photos, doubles are for Ruthel

Maybe Erna was just too busy to socialize. Although her request for a baby carriage is the only allusion to a pregnancy in her correspondence, Erna had three children in three years. Walter and Erna's first son was born on March 6, 1932. He was named Alberto but called Tito from the very start. Their second son, Rodolfo (Rudy), was born only fourteen months later in May 1933. Daughter Helen arrived in July 1934. Even with nannies to help, she had her hands full.

From Erna (Lustig) Neisser to her sister-in-law, Erna (Neisser) Liebermann

Written July 1932, revised in July and sent in August
My dear Erna,

Thank you very much for your last two letters. I cannot return the favor and write you in English since my knowledge of that language has not increased although it has in Spanish. I would not embarrass myself but would have to sit for hours over a letter and [your] nephew Tito does not allow that. It's nice that you are learning languages. But also learn Spanish. A beautiful language and maybe one day you'll come to visit us! Save a lot so you can afford a ship's passage!

Tito and I had terrible colds. We've been better the last two days. It's winter here now. At noon we have the warmest sunshine and at other times of the day moist wind from the sea. Outside everything is green. Dear Erna, you claim the [statio] for your camera has not arrived although we thought you had received it long ago, because Mr. Jacobs took the money to send you a new one when he went back. . . . With the last post we received

Erna and Walter with Tito. 1932.

Klaere's [gift] for Tito. Please thank her and I will soon write them and Kaethe and Erich, in detail.

17.VIII.32 ? Tito gives us so much joy. He is so well behaved and laughs so much; sleeps well through the night and I think he will soon get teeth. We are worried about the housing problem. The owner of our apartment has returned from Germany and is going to take some of his furniture back next week because he is taking another house and does not have everything he needs. We want to buy the rest of the furniture but cannot agree because he is asking quite a bit since it was very expensive when he bought it. So we are looking for another furnished apartment. This is a difficult thing for us because Walter has a lot of work and therefore no time to look around and I can't stay away for long, because every 2½ hours I have to be home for Tito. And the distances are not small here.

Write again soon.

Warm greetings from your sister-in-law Erna. Warm greetings to the dear mother and the siblings.

———————————

What was clear from the beginning is that Walter's wife was a huge asset. Erna had class and good taste and carried herself well. Years later, she dressed elegantly, often changing her clothes three times a day. She had some musical training and her evenings with professional musicians were high-quality cultural events. She had a great eye for art objects and became an expert art collector. Her colonial silver collection was a marvel. Walter was the love of her life and the excerpt from the poem read at their wedding by Kaethe in the name of Walter's brother and sisters, the original German in rhymed couplets, is very accurate.

Erna was the support of the house,
Everywhere she was useful,
Admittedly, she was also much in love!
Nature, the woods, the meadows,
Trees, flowers, the sun, forests
She always loved them deeply.

The poem has another line that is accurate. She loved flowers "but tore the insides out of her dolls." Erna was not much interested in her children.

Walter was a poet with great imagination,
He could compose the most beautiful stories
And knew how to tell them as if they had really happened.
He always raved enormously
About foreign lands and adventures,
The boy just ran away from his parents,
He got all the way to Austria
Then they took him by the ear
And brought him back to the dear parents' home.

═══════════

From Erna (Lustig) Neisser to her mother-in-law Martha (Nothmann) Neisser

28 October 1932

My dear mother,

First of all, I sincerely thank you for the loving wishes for my birthday. Your letter was the only one that arrived exactly on time.

All the others came late. The day went by like all other days of the year. Walter claimed he had not given me a present. But just at that time, he brought me something new to decorate our house almost every day. We received your kind letter from [?] with the last post. Hopefully you have recovered well and were in good company. Walter thanks you for the greetings from Mrs. Erna Schekurst? Please return the greetings when you can. We were once close friends.

My birthday went by quietly because Tito was sick. He has a nasty cold and has still not completely recovered from it. The climate is treacherous. If you get a cold, it's hard to shake. I went through the same last year. When Tito drinks, he already holds his bottle with both hands very well. He eats his porridge at lunch and dinner and his appetite is very good. If one holds out a hand, he hits it alternately with [the right and the left] hand and the louder it sounds, the more he likes it. You were right when you wrote me he would gain weight in a few months. He is cute, plump and has dimples in several places. He is friendly to everyone.

You will have certainly heard that the Rudy Lustigs are going back to Europe. It is very unlikely they will ever come back to Lima. I'm sorry they did not get to see our Tito because they could have talked about him when they got over there [Germany]. We are anxious to know where they will go from Europe.

I'm going to stop for today. Greetings for my dear siblings, my dear parents and in particular, warm greetings and kisses from

your good daughter Erna.

[Walter's postscript to Erna's letter] Dear Mother! Not much has happened here and business continues to be [?]. Sales have not been good and summer is now beginning. Nevertheless, I hope it will get better and quiet, and more pleasant times will come again. [You are starting] the winter season, so I hope business will be good.

From Walter to his sister Erna

> 12 January 1933, Lima
> Letterhead Neisser & Co. Lima P.O. 597 Telephone 30318
> Mercaderes 432/430 Cables NEISSER Lima

Dear little Erna,

Sorry if your birthday was not given the worthy attention it deserves, but my whole family has been sick, so I had to take a lot more time than I intended. Now Erna has gotten rid of her typhoid fever and our Tito is in great shape. To convince you, I'm sending some photos today and I hope you'll be satisfied with them . . .

From Erna (Lustig) Neisser to her sister-in-law Kaethe (Neisser) Simenauer

> 25 February 1933, Lima
> Casilla 597

My dear Kaethe!

Let me congratulate you today on your forthcoming [thirtieth] birthday and wish you all the very best for the coming year and the future. Maybe we can celebrate your next birthday together and your little nephew can congratulate you in person. Just a little while ago I had a funny experience. One should write down all one's experiences immediately because you forget about them after a time. Here it is now the middle of the summer and, which is quite rare—a lot of fog. Not at all healthy for young children. We now see animals that you don't see otherwise, like for example earthworms. My cook called me to come see, [her voice] full of fear. Out in the garden there was a small snake. I hurry out—armed with a stick in order to murder if necessary, and lo and behold—it is a harmless earthworm!

We received such nice photos of you, Erna, and a gentleman (Caballero). You look great in the pictures!

For today, I want to close with a request to write us soon again even if you are very busy. Warm greetings to you, your dear boss, his wife and daughters.

From your good sister Erna

[Walter's postscript to Erna's letter] Dear Kaethe! On your upcoming birthday, my sincere congratulations. Even though you will be another year older and still without an engagement announcement. Anyway, I wish you the very best. Spend your birthday very very pleasantly and celebrate it in accordance with your age. (How old are you really? Pardon me! How young?) Greetings to the entire Mischpoche from me. Let us hear from you again and warm greetings

from your brother Walter

Walter with Rudy and Tito.

Rudy, Helen, and Tito. Lima, 1934.

What Erna does not write about is also of interest. Although only one letter refers to political events, this was a time of brutal repression in Peru, and tens of thousands of members of the left-wing political party APRA (Alianza Popular Revolucionaria Americana) were executed or imprisoned. Erna also fails to mention Walter's business. By October 1931, one year after their marriage, Walter and two partners had sufficient capital to start a business, buying Kussel and Guevara, a store in Lima that had gone bankrupt. The store's inventory included household appliances, lamps, and motors. We know that one of the partners was Ernst Sommerfeld, like Walter a German Jew, but we don't know why Walter bought out his partners so quickly. Erna's January 1933 letter carries the new letterhead that shows the next step. In 1932 Walter created his own company, called Neisser and Co., specialists in machinery and electrical materials.

Kussel and Guevara, the store Walter bought with two partners.
Something in the window attracted a crowd.

In a three-year period between 1930 and 1933, Walter's personal and work life changed dramatically. He started in Peru as an employee of the AEG subsidiary Ferrostaal and managed to buy a company in 1931, but one year later he had shaken off his partners and started his own business.

During these years Walter finessed an extraordinary arrangement with the Peruvian government. First, Neisser and Co. became the Westinghouse representative for Peru; next, Neisser and Westinghouse became the sole providers of electrical power bought by the state. When it came to government contracts, the other companies that sold the same equipment were not even in the running. Every new turbine, every new electrical plant, and to a great extent almost every new refrigerator, stove, and lamp went through his company. For a period of twenty years, from 1933 to the early 1950s, the money poured in. How and why and especially with whom Walter made this arrangement is unclear. Someone high up in government circles, someone with a great deal of power, set up and benefited from this agreement. It may be a possibility that this person was also a member of the Masons.

At first business was good, then spectacularly successful. An expanding population and increased urbanization favored Walter's enterprise. Although these were the early years of the Depression, US capital increased sharply and there was an upsurge of the progressive sectors of Peruvian society over the old landholding class, developments that were favorable to new businesses. Neisser and Co. thrived and Walter became very prosperous in a short time.

CHAPTER FOUR

Ruth Actively Coordinated the Paperwork with Walter

The Arrival of Walter's Family, 1933–1940

THE National Socialists, with Hitler as their leader, came to power in 1933. In Germany xenophobia raged and Jews were targeted. The passage of the Nuremberg Laws two years later severely curtailed the lives of German Jews: Professionals were no longer allowed to practice, students were denied access to schools, and merchants lost their clients to German boycotts. Every month brought new restrictions.

Walter closely followed the political events in Nazi Germany and their dire consequences for his family. From his vantage point in Peru, he could see the deterioration as middle-class merchant families like the Neissers became poor and frightened, then hungry and desperate. He did not sit idly by. In less than seven years, he managed the impossible: He brought almost all of his immediate and extended family to Lima.

In the early 1930s Walter was probably almost as concerned about the situation in Peru. The Great Depression had devastated the economy, and as a producer of primary products, Peru suffered greatly. Copper exports to the United States and Germany decreased by more than 50 percent, and as prices dropped, debt mounted. With the new Peruvian currency, the sol de oro, slipping in value, many export companies went bankrupt, salaries fell, and workers went on strike.

Although Peru exported less during this period, it was one of the only South American countries not to restrict imports, allowing Walter, who represented many foreign companies, to cement his future. His son Rudy writes: "Neisser and Co. was the only company [in Peru] to sell electrical equipment to the state. [My father's] friendship with Empresas Eléctricas [the national electric company] was such that he monopolized the use of electricity. Walter Neisser was a tiger when it came to business." We do not know how Walter obtained his undeclared monopoly. In order to make this arrangement and keep it in place, government employees had to be complicit. Perhaps Gotardo Piazza, the Westinghouse agent for all of South America, or Walter's close friend Enrique Torres Bellón, president of the Peruvian Senate, was involved. Walter's relations with the political elite were so cordial that he was invited to their social events. His daughter Helen remembers wearing her first long dress to a presidential function.

Peru's economy was slowly changing. Industry and urbanization were replacing agriculture. As people moved down from the mountains to the coast and settled in Lima, ever-swelling new neighborhoods grew around the city center. The government invested in a large number of public works such as the Chimbote iron and steel works and expanded basic infrastructure, making Neisser and Co. extremely profitable. Between 1933 and 1950, Walter made a fortune.

But immigration laws were beyond Walter's control. It was quite easy to immigrate in 1927 when he arrived in Peru with a contract from a German company. But the governments of two successive presidents, Luis Sánchez Cerro (1931–1933) and Óscar Benavides

(1933–1939), brought in new punitive and restrictive laws concerning immigration and foreign residents. The initial round, passed in 1932, was directed against Japanese businesses, but it affected all foreigners. The first Japanese had arrived in Peru in 1899 to work as farm laborers on the coastal sugar plantations, but after their four-year farm contracts expired, they moved to the cities, opened small businesses, and became very successful, to the dismay of many. By the early 1930s they totaled 33,000, and the government moved to curtail their activity and prevent more Japanese from coming. The 1932 law decreed that 80 percent of the employees of a given company must be Peruvian nationals and that the same percentage must be distributed in salaries—that is, the Peruvian national employees must receive 80 percent of the total amount paid out in salaries.

When President Óscar Benavides came to power in 1933, he was even more punitive than his predecessor. He imposed special taxes on foreign nationals and limited the number of businesses with foreign ownership. In addition, although there were few requests, he established quotas for immigrants and required foreign nationals to register annually. Immigrants needed capital of at least 2,000 soles (over $1,000 US) to be admitted to the country.

The early laws had targeted foreigners who were already Peruvian residents, but by 1936 the demand for visas to enter the country from Japan and Europe had grown much greater. The 1936 immigration laws were meant to further restrict access to Peru. This legislation established new immigration quotas, brought in a specific tax and mandatory annual registration for foreign residents, and again limited the number of licenses available to foreigners to open and operate businesses. Extra measures were taken to keep out immigrants from Japan, but the process became more difficult for everyone. By 1937, the cost of a visa to enter the country had risen

yet again, and immigrants were required to deposit 8,000 soles—
in addition to the 2,000 soles demanded previously—in case they
didn't find work. Those who were still unemployed within two
years of their arrival were to be repatriated. Gypsies and people with
physical and mental disabilities were banned.

Further restrictions in the late 1930s increased the cost of the
visa yet again. Although the legislation was once more intended to
stop Japanese immigrants, its effect was to exclude almost everyone.
In addition, Japanese nationals were prohibited from becoming naturalized Peruvian citizens.

The government showed no interest in Jews until 1938, when
Peruvian consulates received a directive to cease all Jewish immigration. Walter had the means to pay the special taxes, and his
company grew so quickly that he could comply with all the new
restrictions. In the early years, he was quite easily able to supply
almost every relative with a visa for Peru, but he had to overcome
formidable bureaucratic challenges as the rules grew stiffer.

The outcome of the visa application depended on the person
in charge. Although consular officers in Peru and Peruvian embas-
sies and consulates in Europe had orders to refuse Jews after 1938,
some made exceptions—for example, Federico Mould Távara in
Paris granted a great many Jewish requests. But the total number of
visas issued was minute, and a Peruvian visa was essential for leaving
Germany. Without it, the process of securing all of the necessary
official papers could not even begin.

Germany required every emigrant to have at least four documents that were difficult to obtain: an entrance visa to Peru, an exit
visa from Nazi Germany, a travel permit, and by the late 1930s,
a baptismal certificate, a police certificate, and financial information. Jews were issued one-way passports, essentially a travel permit.

Each document had an expiry date, and if applicants didn't succeed in complying with it, they had to start the process all over again. The number of necessary documents rose every year and further papers were sometimes demanded. So many had to be obtained and they were so haphazardly delivered that members of a single family often had to travel separately.

Acquiring an exit visa from Nazi Germany was a costly nightmare that meant standing in line for days. Whether the visa was granted or refused hinged on the whim of the official in charge. Travel permits were also expensive and seemed to be issued at random. As for the baptismal certificate, which became a prerequisite to enter Peru in the late 1930s, Jews bought forged ones or found a priest willing to risk his life since forgery was expressly forbidden.

We do not have a visa for anyone in the Neisser family, but we have several related documents, including my mother's travel document from Karlsbad, in what later became the Czech Republic. (She met my father in Peru.) Her J Reisepass, Jewish travel permit, number 2855, is dated October 6, 1939, and the letter J is the largest script on the page. At the top it says "Deutsches Reich" (German Reich), followed by the eagle and swastika. Her name is given as Gertrude Sara Neubauer, because the Nazis automatically added "Sara" to every Jewish female

Travel permit (Reisepass) for my mother, Gertrude Neubauer.

name. (Every male was forced to bear the name "Israel.") Below "citizenship," given again as "German Reich," it says "Protectorate of Bohemia and Moravia (Protektorat Böhmen und Mähren)."

In addition, we have copies of two forged black-market Peruvian tourist visas bought in Germany. Gaby Klehmann Winter, a friend from Peru, shared these documents. Her parents, Guenther and Tamara, arrived in the southern Peruvian port of Mollendo in January 1939. The number of seals, stamps, and written notes on the German part of the passport attest to the difficulties in obtaining it. The Peruvian visa specifically states that the bearer must leave the country after the time allotted, a mere two months. When Gaby sent me the documents, she said that she knew Walter Neisser had intervened on her parents' behalf and his actions had permitted her parents to remain in Peru. She had no further details.

———

The visa for Tamara Klehmann reads:

Valid for foreign countries from 11/21/38 to 12/31/1939
[Breslau] Wroclaw, the 21 Nov. 1938 / The chief of police /
To order: [illegible].
TOURIST
SEEN AT THE CONSULATE [illegible]
VALID FOR ENTRY TO Perú by Mollendo via Cuzco [handwritten]
PARIS November 26, 1938 [handwritten]
Authorized by the Consul of Perú, signed in his name by [handwritten, signature illegible] Chancellor
The tourist is traveling together with her husband, to whom a visa was issued in his passport on September 7 of this year. Second-class

return tickets have been shown and a statement that they intend to return to their country is attached; medical and financial statements as well as a criminal background check. This visa is valid for only a two-month stay in Perú. [handwritten]

Seal: Consulate General of Perú in France–Paris and stamp

Order #: [illegible]

Tax #: [illegible]

Fee Paid: 20 soles

Tourist visa for Tamara Klehmann.

The visa for Guenther Klehmann reads:

Tourist, Seen at the consulate for Peru
Valid for entry to Peru via Mollendo, via Cuzco, Paris
November 26, 1938
Authorized by the consul of Peru [signature illegible],
Chancellor

Tourist. He is accompanied by his wife who was issued a visa in her passport dated 7 September. He has presented a roundtrip ticket in 2nd class. A statement that he intends to return to his country; medical, financial as well as a criminal background check. Visa only valid for a two-month stay in Peru. [handwritten]

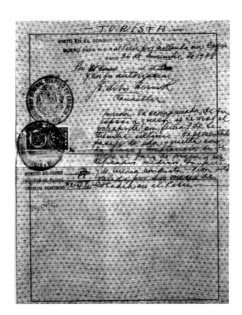

Peruvian tourist visa for Guenther Klehmann.

The fallback option for the Klehmanns was to go on to Bolivia, the only country that accepted refugees. In fact the Bolivian experience is completely different from that of all the other countries in the Americas. Bolivia did not discriminate. According to Leo Spitzer in *Hotel Bolivia*, Bolivia was still accepting Jewish refugees when the war began, and once it ended welcomed many Nazis, among them Klaus Barbie. (During the war years, the Atlantic Ocean carried only warships and there was no contact between combatants. Mail delivery halted and no immigrants arrived.) Although the numbers vary with the sources, approximately 20,000 German Jews entered Bolivia between 1937 and 1940. This figure is larger than the combined figures for Canada, Australia, New Zealand, South Africa, and India.

Walter's family began arriving in 1933. His only brother, Erich, and little sister, Erna, were the first to come. His sister Kaethe came three years later, his mother in 1937, and his oldest sister Klaere on one of the last boats in 1940. In addition, Walter's mother's relatives, more than thirty members of the Nothmann family, emigrated either alone or with members of their immediate families. Relatives arrived every single year between 1933 and 1940.

In July of 1933, Walter's wife Erna wrote to her mother-in-law asking that one of Walter's sisters come to Lima to help her care for her two small children. We do not know whether the situation in Germany played any role in this request.

From Erna (Lustig) Neisser to her mother-in-law Martha (Nothmann) Neisser

21 July 1933, Lima
Letterhead Neisser & Co. SPECIALIST IN MACHINERY
AND ELECTRICAL MATERIAL

My dear Mother,

Thank you very much for the dear airmail lines from you, the Freund family and Erich. We're doing quite well except for Tito, who has a cold. Rudy is back in shape and is gaining weight well and is sweet, round and roly-poly.

Walter with his two sons.

Today, Walter and I have a suggestion to make: If Erna or Kaethe would care to become our nursemaid or infant caregiver (but taken seriously), we would appreciate if you could give one of them the permission to do so. It would be good if she sat in at a baby nursery for a 1-month orientation period to get some guidance. The smock for the job, bed linens, bath linens, (warm coat), sports dress for tennis, 2 nice simple housedresses, for the winter woolen clothes like over there [Germany] and don't forget a knitted vest and woolen slippers. To go out, the same kind of clothes as over there. No rainwear or overshoes. Umbrellas are impossible! The same is true for Erich.

We wanted to make this proposal a long time ago, but lacked company for the young lady on the long journey. Now we have that [because Erich is making the trip], and all that is missing is your consent. We are convinced that Erna or Kaethe would like to come and also that they will carry out their duties conscientiously. Of course, this profession takes a lot of patience. It's nice to be out in the fresh air, rather than sitting in between 4 walls and waiting for a customer to come. For you, dear mother, it is not an easy decision to be separated for such a long time from one of your daughters. It will not be a very long stay since our sons must meet their grandparents; thus, there is an excellent chance the return trip will take place soon. Now, dear mother, don't think about it for long and decide quickly; generous as you are always are, just say Yes.

Erich should bring: clothes like you wear over there. Not too much because everything is cheap here; 1-2 linen suits (white). In Panama, he can add the bath linens, bed linens, towels. He should bring novel gifts and household items on sale.

For me, please send: 1 white or light-colored knitted wool vest, collarless [. . .]; from Father Lustig 3 pairs of English wool socks, gray, size 10½. For Tito woolen and (Nado) outfits and wool-pile socks. For me, one sport coat in brushed wool, size 44, light taupe color if available on sale at the end of the season, a wool muslin sun dress that does not wrinkle, 1 pair [. . .] colored Salamander shoes, size 5½ with the dark brown heels 12, 4½ cm high (please quite large).

For today, I want to close with the warmest regards and kisses for you and the dear siblings.

Your good daughter Erna

[Walter continues.]

Dear Mother,

Unfortunately, it is now too late to write anything. I'll do this with the next post. Warm greetings to all. Your guilty son Walter

[Postscript from Walter.] Don't do anything about passports, etc. I will write about steamers, etc. The local Ministry of Foreign Affairs will write to the general [Last line on side not legible].
[Postscript from Erna.] Get vaccinated against typhoid.

━━━━━━━━━

Walter's note in the margin of this letter indicates that he will take care of the paperwork, contact a general, and check on boats. Presumably the general was the contact who facilitated the Peruvian visas. It is clear that Walter had help from one or more people in Lima. In the fall of 1933, a few months after Erna wrote this letter, help arrived in the person of Walter's youngest sister, Erna, the recipient of so many letters. My father, his brother Erich, accompanied her to Lima.

Walter's sister Kleine Erna is seated at the far right. Beside her is Walter with Tito in his lap. Further to the left, his wife Erna holds Helen. Lima, late 1934 or early 1935.

As they arrived, Walter integrated the family members into his business. My father, Erich, had worked in stores in both Beuthen and Gleiwitz, but he had lost his job for the double sin of being a Jew and a socialist. He had helped his mother for a while, but as son number three, he could more easily fly under the parental radar. In Lima Walter immediately employed both him and his sister, one in the business, the other in the home, establishing a precedent for all the relatives who followed. Neither lasted; Erna took care of Walter's children for just two years. Until his marriage in 1940, Erich did not have great needs, and everyone agrees that he did not exert himself. In Peru, he worked in the paper industry, first selling imported paper and paper bags, later expanding to everything related to stationery and school supplies. In an era before the advent of the plastic bag, everything was sold in brown paper bags of different sizes and different weights, and Erich enjoyed the freedom of the salesman, selling enough to get by.

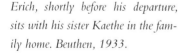

Erich, shortly before his departure, sits with his sister Kaethe in the family home. Beuthen, 1933.

My father was the antithesis of his brother. He had none of his drive, none of his easy charm, none of his business acumen. He certainly lacked Walter's facility with languages. He was kind, selfless, and uninterested in amassing wealth. Where Walter was the center of every gathering, Erich hid in the wings. Although Erich was a good salesman, he was probably more successful as a Jewish community volunteer for the new immigrants who arrived shortly after him. Because his time was very much his own, he was one of several people who met the boats that arrived from Europe, ushered people through customs, greased palms, and smoothed the feathers of the customs officers.

My mother's favorite story, and the only war story she told because it was a happy one, was of her arrival in December 1939. As she prepared to disembark in Callao, customs officials stopped

her and challenged her baptismal certificate—with good reason since it was dated 1939. Luckily two community volunteers, Erich and his cousin Herbert Nothmann, were at hand. Erich told her to start speaking German, to say the word Christ as often as possible, to make it sound like prayer, and to cross herself repeatedly. Most likely a bribe was paid. After she made it through customs, she realized that her suitcase had been stolen, and her only possessions

Kleine Erna in front of a clothing store. Germany, 1935.

were her purse and the clothes on her back. The happy outcome of that encounter was the wedding, some ten months later, of my parents, Erich Neisser and Trude Neubauer.

Kleine Erna, the youngest of seven children, was twelve years younger than Walter and fifteen years younger than her oldest sister, Klaere. Erna was closer in age to Klaere's daughter Ruth, and she and Ruth were constant companions throughout their lives, more like sisters than aunt and niece. It is telling that in Walter and Erna's wedding picture, Kleine Erna and Ruth stand together in the very top row wearing matching white blouses and little bow ties. Presumably the older siblings had doted on Erna when she was small, because they doted on her when she lived in Lima. Erna was sickly—she probably had tuberculosis, and I remember she had only one lung. This may have been why she and her husband had just one child, Miguel / Michael.

In 1935, Erna went back to Germany with Walter and his family to find a husband. After a short time she returned to Peru with Heinz Liebermann, his parents, and his brother. Aside from her short stint as a nanny, Erna never worked and never seemed to venture far from her small living room where family members visited constantly. She sat at the table with her stamp collection, took care of her fish tank and turtle, and raised succeeding generations of cats who were always called Max. Despite her bad lung, she and almost everyone else smoked.

Erna's husband Heinz immediately started work at Neisser and Co. and that is where he stayed until his retirement. He was the only member of the family who was a store manager. Everyone else who worked at Neisser and Co. took on more responsible managerial positions, but Heinz remained in the Callao store from the time it opened in the forties until it closed in the sixties.

Callao, Lima's port, some twenty kilometers from downtown, is a shabby, dirty city, like all ports known less for its culture and glamour than for its sailors and seedy areas. The Neisser store had the usual array of washing machines, stoves and refrigerators, lamps and small appliances. Managing it was not hard; more than anything, it required someone who was honest and could watch over a few employees. At one point Walter tried moving Heinz to a bigger store, but it did not work out and Walter shipped him right back to Callao.

The Neisser store that Heinz managed. Lima Street, Callao.

Although his brother and little sister were not much help, the early years saw the arrival of two cousins, Herbert and Curt Nothmann, who were crucial to the early growth of the company. The Westinghouse representation permitted Walter to sell and install not only power plants throughout the country but also appliances. The first store, on Mantas Street half a block from the Plaza de Armas,

Lima's main square, sold household appliances big and small, lamps, and some machinery. In addition, Walter successfully negotiated with other foreign companies to represent and distribute American and European products. The business expanded as more relatives arrived. By the early forties, Neisser and Co. had four stores in Lima. Cousin Ulrich (Ulli) Neisser would eventually manage a fifth in Arequipa.

Walter's sister Kaethe and her husband, Wilhelm Simenauer, always called Sim, arrived in 1936. Kaethe carefully documented their Atlantic crossing in her photo album. They boarded a steamer called the *Hindenburg* on January 31, stopped in Antwerp, and continued on a second ship, the *Amasis*. She included pictures of her newborn baby, Ursula, fellow passengers, and the Panama Canal. The couple's second daughter, Vera, was born in Lima in 1939.

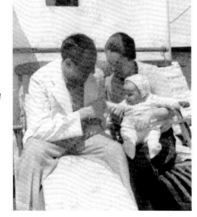

Sim, Kaethe, and Ursula on board the Amasis. *1936.*

Kaethe and Sim were quite different from Erna and Heinz. At first they both worked for Walter at Neisser and Co., but in 1948 they made a special arrangement to open first one and soon after a second independent store called Neisser Regalos (Gifts). They carried similar wares but specialized in luxury items for grand

The first sticker says "Ueberfahrt 36" (crossing) and the name of the boat.
The second says, "Der Panama Kanal."

occasions, such as weddings. They kept the well-known Neisser name without being part of the chain. Walter was their partner and financial backer. After his death, Grosse Erna tried to withdraw the bank guarantees extended to Neisser Regalos, but Sim had such a fit that she relented.

The inauguration of Kaethe and Sim's store in 1948. Walter is in the center, Erna wearing one of her signature hats to his left; the children's nanny Thea (Hirsch) Kahn and Sim to his right.

Kaethe was an elegant businesswoman who spent her days in the store. With her dyed red hair, red fingernails, tailored suits, and high-heeled shoes, she always looked ready to go to work and always seemed unhappy. I don't ever remember seeing her without high heels, for even her slippers had heels. She consistently ate salads and fruits and never gained weight.

The year 1937 saw the arrival of the mothers, both recently widowed: Walter's mother, Martha Nothmann Neisser, aged sixty-four years, and Erna's mother, Fanny Lanzer Lustig, aged sixty years, traveled together to Peru. I thought they would have been glad to leave Germany, but the letter written six months after Fanny's arrival shows that was not the case.

Kaethe at the far right, her husband Sim at the far left, and Walter in the dinner jacket.

═══════════

Fanny Lustig to her sister-in-law Lina (Helene Weiss) in Glei-witz, Germany

22 March 1938

. . . Now dear Lina I will tell you my decision and the conclusion of dear Erna. I am not so indifferent when I tell you this. Since the climate and the E (?) suit me well, I have decided to remain here for good. Now I ask you, dear Lina, dear Lucy and Fritz and Salka to liquidate my apartment . . .

═══════════

Because it was obvious that both mothers could not live with Walter and his family, Walter provided his mother with a small house only a block from his own. She shared her Miraflores home with a dog, a

With palm trees in the background, Martha Neisser and Fanny Lustig pose with their children and grandchildren shortly after their arrival. Top row: Martha, Sim, Fanny, Kaethe. Bottom row: Ursula, Kleine Erna, Helen, Rudy, Tito.

Erna's mother, Fanny Lustig (left), and Walter's mother, Martha Neisser. Lima, 1937.

When this beautifully composed picture was taken, the tight family circle was almost complete. Martha Neisser stands in the middle, her daughter Kaethe to the far left, daughter Erna in the door frame. Her oldest granddaughter, Ruth Angress, and Ruth's husband, Kurt, stand on either side of her. Five grandchildren—Kaethe's children, Vera and Ursula, and Walter's, Rudy, Helen, and Tito—are in front.

Pekinese called Tai, and a servant, Irene. Additional help came from a neighbor, also from Upper Silesia, whom we called Tante Grete although she was not our aunt. There were always candies on the table and visitors on the terrace, which faced the narrow garden. Martha's brothers, sister, in-laws, children, and grandchildren all lived within walking distance. How well she adapted is unclear, although she no doubt understood how very fortunate she was. She had no financial worries, and her children came to her house every Friday evening and any time there was an occasion to celebrate. For me she made hot *Pfannkuchen*, deep-fried doughnuts filled with jam.

Walter's daughter Helen writes: "I was around four years old when my grandmothers arrived by boat. We went to Callao where we received them with flowers and the children read poems. From then on the Sabbath was observed. We called my mother's mother Omi and everyone else called her Omi Lustig. She lived with us and she lit candles on Friday evening and prayed in both Hebrew and German. She observed the Sabbath strictly, never got in a car, not even to go to synagogue, for those twenty-four hours."

Walter's older sister, Klaere, and her husband, Friedrich Freund, arrived in Lima in January 1940. Klaere died within a year during an operation to alleviate the discomfort of her severe varicose veins. No one knew why, and the question, much discussed by family members, was never really resolved. As the eldest daughter, Klaere had been very close to her mother, and her death at age forty-seven was an unexpected blow.

Klaere's husband immediately joined Neisser and Co., but it must have been very difficult for him to become Walter's employee. In the 1920s and early 1930s, Friedrich Freund had owned a clothing store on the main square in Beuthen. It was a large enterprise, several stories high, with professionally decorated window displays.

Klaere (Neisser) Freund and her husband Friedrich Freund just after their arrival in Lima (their boat is visible in the background). The family is all dressed up to greet them, the women in hats, Erich in a white linen suit. From left, Erich, Ruth, Friedrich Freund, Kaethe, Martha, Klaere, and Sim. The little girls are Helen, Moritz's granddaughter Liliana (Nothmann) Orsero, and Ursula.

He sold mostly high-end clothing for adults and children, outerwear, ski outfits, and silk stockings. Active in the local community, he was extremely enterprising—head of the local B'nai Brith lodge, on the board of various Jewish organizations in Upper Silesia, and the recipient of an Iron Cross for his service in the First World War. Klaere had stayed at home with her only child. Ruth, born in 1915, studied business in Berlin, and joined her father in the store. Klaere's grandson Ronny Angress, born in Lima three years after his grandmother's death, adds that his grandfather had some shrapnel circulating in his body that eventually reached his heart and killed him.

Friedrich Freund wearing his First World War medals, the Iron Cross around his neck.   *Friedrich Freund's store window in Beuthen with an outstanding array of manikin legs to display the silk stockings.*

After Klaere's death, Friedrich remarried. With women who were both Jewish and German-speaking in short supply in Lima, he found a wife within the family circle. She was Klaere and Walter's cousin, Erna Nothmann, who bore what must have been a very popular name at the time. She had divorced her first husband, also a Nothmann, and after Friedrich Freund's death, she, in turn, married for a third time, luckily finding someone outside the family, Bondy Emoedy, a wonderful Hungarian Jew who spoke German.

Klaere and Friedrich's daughter Ruth and her husband Kurt Angress had come to Lima two years before, and Ruth had of course joined Neisser and Co. Ronny Angress writes, "My parents arrived in 1938. . . . My mother mentioned a couple of times that she worked actively to coordinate their paperwork with Walter. They also worked on Kurt's parents' papers, but they only got as far as Colombia."

Walter's letters from the 1920s mention nothing remotely Jewish, but once his family joined him in Lima, Walter began to participate in the community, all the while remaining active in the Masons and the Rotarians and pursuing his many business interests. Lima had changed since his arrival in 1927. There were more German-speaking Jews, although the numbers were still minuscule—fourteen families arrived in 1933, twenty-two in 1934, and only thirty-five in 1935. Only then were there enough people to create an organization, whereas the Sephardic community had had one since 1922 and the Yiddish-speaking Ashkenazim since 1923. There was no talk of cooperation among the three groups because they spoke different languages, had different backgrounds, and typically didn't mix.

Walter was one of the founders of the new German-Jewish self-help organization, known initially as the Hilfsverein (aid union) in German and in Spanish as the Jewish German-Speaking Mutual Aid Society (Sociedad Israelita de Socorros Mutuos de Judíos de Habla Alemana). In 1938 it became the Sociedad de Beneficiencia Israelita de 1870, and to this day is called "La 1870." The name and the date were chosen to honor an earlier organization developed by nineteenth-century Jewish immigrants who had left when the war over saltpeter sent the economy into a tailspin. This early organization planned to build a synagogue, create a school, and found a cemetery, but only the last of their goals came to fruition. The members bought land and created the first Jewish cemetery in Latin America. The figures for the cemetery speak for themselves. In the eighty-three years between the founding of the cemetery and Hitler's rise to power (1850–1933), only some 214 people were buried, with perhaps 100 more not recorded.

In 1935, Walter served as secretary of La 1870 and cousin Herbert Nothmann became treasurer. Over the next ten years, Walter and other members of the family took turns at all the executive positions. In addition to functioning as a self-help society, La 1870 organized services for the High Holidays. The first year, 1935, saw twelve people attend in a private home. Later both the cemetery and care for the sick were part of their mandate. In about 1937 the community in Peru received a *sefer torah* from Beuthen, the town where many members of the Neisser and Nothmann families had resided. It would be interesting to know who guided it on its long journey.

The former world of the Neissers and Nothmanns had disappeared. They now lived in a coastal city where mangos and avocados were plentiful. To the east rose the treeless, towering Andes; to the south and north, there were sandy deserts. At twilight the sun disappeared into the Pacific Ocean, the language on the street was Spanish, the religion Roman Catholic. In Peru there were huge racial and class distinctions, and great poverty was common. Garbage filled the streets, some of which still had open sewers. Even the seasons were reversed. The contrast between the photograph taken at my parents' wedding in 1940 and Walter and Erna's formal wedding picture taken in 1930 mirrors the transformation.

Walter had long since come to terms with the Peruvian reality and saw only possibilities. For him the untold potential he had described on his first visit to Germany had become real and he worked relentlessly to make the rest of the family embrace his dream. Not only had he obtained the visas, but he had convinced them all to come. Perhaps to that end he had made two trips to Germany, although he was a businessman first and foremost and was pursuing his business interests at the same time. In 1935, just five years after his marriage, his financial situation had changed so dramatically that he had sufficient funds to take his wife, children, and little sister to visit the family. Grosse Erna wanted to see her parents

This picture was taken on September 1, 1940, the wedding day of my parents, Erich Neisser and Trude Neubauer, almost exactly ten years after Walter and Erna were married. Walter has brought all the members of his immediate family to Lima. In the front row from left are Walter, Tito, Helen, Vera, Rudy, Ursula, and Erich. In row 2 are Friedrich Freund, Klaere, Martha, Kaethe, Sim, and Kurt Angress. My mother (the bride, Trude Neubauer) and Fanny Lustig are in the third row. In row 4 are Thea Nothmann, ?, Ruth Angress, and Kleine Erna. Guenter Nothmann stands at the rear.

and introduce them to her children, and her young sons needed treatment for asthma, enabling Erna and the children to spend time at a spa in the Tatra mountains south of Gleiwitz and Beuthen.

Walter was also rich enough to afford a nanny. Since neither Kleine nor Grosse Erna had shown much interest in child care, Walter placed an advertisement in the local Gleiwitz newspaper, and in 1936 Walter's wife and children returned to Lima with the capable and efficient Thea Hirsch, the nanny who stayed with the family until her marriage to Max Kahn several years later. Eventually Walter moved her into the business. His ability to measure a person's potential was a key element in his success.

Walter traveling with his children. 1935.

Kleine Erna, Ruth and Kurt Angress, Grosse Erna, Thea (Hirsch) Kahn, and Walter's children. 1935.

An outing at the spa. Germany, 1935.

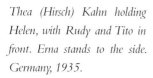

Thea (Hirsch) Kahn holding Helen, with Rudy and Tito in front. Erna stands to the side. Germany, 1935.

On his second trip two years later, Walter stopped to do business in New York both going and coming, and in Germany he recruited personnel for the company. One of the people he hired was Wilhelm Badrian Frey, an electrical engineer and a Gleiwitz resident. In Upper Silesia, Badrian had been in charge of the installation of the high-voltage lines that supplied electrical power to the arms and munitions factories in the area. Since he was Jewish, Badrian thought it prudent to leave. He signed a contract with Neisser and Co. and quietly began to complete the paperwork required. He arrived in Lima with his wife and son Guenther in July 1937.

We have no record of Walter's intentions, but it seems likely that one of the underlying reasons for these German trips was that he was trying to persuade reluctant family members to leave the country. In 1935 German Jews were still convinced that Hitler's government would not last and Hitler was but a passing political problem. They believed that Upper Silesia was far enough away from Berlin that their isolation would protect them. The many First World War veterans in the family, who had fought bravely and won medals, could not imagine that they would face the kind of discrimination that would follow.

But because the situation in Germany had seriously deteriorated, Walter urged family members to speed up their departure plans. About this trip Walter's daughter Helen writes: "The situation in Germany was already very tense in the years before the war and signs of Nazi presence were evident in the streets. The Nazi salute, right arm extended and a 'Heil Hitler,' was mandatory at the time and my father refused to use that greeting. Since he had been in South America for many years and spoke good Spanish, he would pretend not to understand German. He would answer in Spanish in order not to salute." Walter's behavior in the face of the Nazi danger was risky, perhaps even foolhardy, but it was also admirable.

CHAPTER FIVE

You, Dear Fanny, Can Thank God You Are Out

Letters from Germany, 1937–1940

WHEN Walter returned to Peru, he wanted to show the members of La 1870 the movies he had taken on his second trip to Germany, but they were not receptive. As soon as the reel began, they asked him to turn off the projector. Although the community members did not want to see the events unfolding in Germany, the correspondence that follows—the letters Walter's mother-in-law received in Lima—brings them vividly to light.

From the time of her arrival in Peru in 1937 until her death in 1955, Walter's mother-in-law, Fanny Lustig, lived with Walter's family. And that is the reason we have her letters. When Walter's big house was sold, her grandchildren found and kept them, and when we planned a family history, they sent them to me. All date from the late 1930s, immediately after her arrival in Lima. She would certainly not have shared their contents with her grandchildren, who were under ten years old. Helen remembers how Fanny wept over the letters and read them again and again. Helen and her siblings read them for the first time seventy years later.

Fanny Lustig, shortly after her arrival, poses with her three grandchildren. Lima, 1937.

Many of the details we have about the conditions in Gleiwitz after Fanny's departure come from the letters, which cover a three-year period that ended abruptly in 1940. Most of her correspondents—sisters-in-law, nieces, nephews, and cousins, as well as the people mentioned in the letters—did not come to Peru. The Neisser family had the good fortune to have Walter, who was committed to bringing them to Peru, but the Lustigs scattered. A few came to Peru; others went to Argentina with the help of Rudy Lustig, who has already played a big role in this story. Some went to Shanghai, some to England, some to the United States. The others perished.

We have no photographs from the period, but of course many Lustigs attended Walter and Erna's wedding and appear in their wedding picture. Fanny Lustig, the mother of the bride, had a place of honor seated at Walter's right, front and center. Her only daughter was finally getting married and she was enjoying herself. At the time of the wedding, her husband Salomon (affectionately called Sally) was still alive. He is seated beside Walter's mother, Martha, to the left of the bride and groom.

The many people named below, all members of the Lustig family, have surnames, given names, and nicknames, much like characters in a Russian novel. Because I met only those who came to Lima, the rest are impossible for me to keep straight. The Lustig family tree includes three Klaras, two with a *K* and one with a *C*, all in the same generation; three Fannys; three Fritzes; several Maxes; an Else and an Ilse. Salomon's sisters, Lina and Clara, both married men called Weiss. In addition, the letter writers could well have used spellings that are different from the spelling on my copy of the Lustig family tree. On the other hand, Kurt Berger, who is mentioned several times, is very much a known entity. His wife, Margot, Fanny's beloved niece, her parents, and their two sons came to Lima, and several worked for Walter. Kurt arrived before his wife and many years before his children. A letter from Margot, written while she was waiting for her papers, is included here.

Walter's mother-in-law had many names. In the letters, she is addressed as Franziska, her full name; Fanny, her nickname; and Saline, a shortening of her husband's name, Salomon. Another quirk is that several letters have multiple authors, a common practice at the time. The first letter was written by three people.

━━━━━━━

From Fanny Lustig's niece Clara Lustig, her sister-in-law Fanny Glaser, and her nephew Wilhelm Lustig to Fanny Lustig

Chanukkah, 1937, Gleiwitz

Dear Aunt Saline,

I am happy to be able to send you a few words. To our joy, we heard that the two Omas [grandmothers] had withstood the journey across the big waters well. Now we hope that we will soon receive a detailed report from you and promise we will answer immediately.

Please greet all your loved ones. (Erna must be on her way to the U.S.A.) I hope you will be well and I send you heartfelt greetings from your niece.

Clara

Dear Franziska,

Every day we think a long letter from you might arrive. Most importantly you are feeling well and your children are bringing you joy. We heard about your arrival from Beuthen. We are feeling well in our new quarters. Lilien/Lieschen has visited me every day for almost a year. Everything else is in order.

Clara [Klara Weiss, Lina's sister] is going to call us; she had to have an operation. We hope she will be better. Again best wishes for you and your children. I remain your devoted sister,

Fanny Glaser

[Wilhelm's part of the letter is one of the few that nobody could decipher. It was tackled by all my helpers and all declared it impossible to read.]

━━━━━━━

Fanny Lustig's main correspondent is her sister-in-law Helene Weiss, the sister of her husband Salomon (Sally). An old lady living in a Gleiwitz retirement home, she is known by her nickname, Lina. In her three letters, Lina gives eloquent descriptions of the tightening noose of Nazi regulations and how they affected daily life. In one letter she mentions Walter's visit, what he did, and what they talked about. She does not admit how hard up she is until late in her letter when she lists the debts she is trying to collect, the household furniture she has sold, and the amounts she has received. The letters had to get past the censors, and Lina is circumspect in her criticism of the regime. Finally, it is curious that Lina waits until the very end of this letter to mention Sally's unveiling, an important graveside service to mark the end of the mourning period for Salomon. The fact that she says nothing, except that everyone attended, is perhaps a poignant barb at Fanny, the widow now in Lima, not present at her own husband's unveiling. From the Lustig family tree, we know Lina died in 1940.

━━━━━━━━━━

From Lina (Helene Weiss) to her sister-in-law Fanny Lustig, with a postscript from her cousin Ida [Neumann?]

7 December 1937, Gleiwitz

My dear Fanny,

You cannot imagine with what longing we received your dear letter on the 3.12. We were all very happy about it because you write us only good things. I would have liked to have been at that welcome. We talked about you every day. Erna must already have joined Walter. He told us that she would meet him in New York. I hope they look up Georg. I asked them to because it has been a long time since I received a letter [from him] and now many weeks have passed and again I have no news even though I have written 1 letter and 2 cards.

Walter only spent ¼ hour with me. I gave him the mushrooms and he fetched the stamps from the house himself. Paula [a niece] was here last month and brought nothing. She complained that Walter drove by her house and did not visit her. I had kept it [her complaints] a secret from Walter. But he said to me, "Calm yourself, dear aunt." Because of that I visited her this time, stayed overnight and did not give Walter anything to take. She wanted to write you and Erna. Has she done so?

I conveyed your greetings to everyone, and they in turn send you the same. When I paid the rent, I also passed on your greetings to Lustig and he asked me to send along the card. Walter told me again I should rent [part of] the apartment but it is hard to find the right person. You can't take in just anyone. I don't know if I wrote you that the Kallmans moved into the house on Kloken Street and that they handed over the back room and the small children's room to the Schweigers. The [Jewish] community placed a small gas stove in the entry so they could cook. I could have had them come to me but they wanted the empty apartment, then did not like the bathtub . . .

We were all at the cemetery for Sally's unveiling. Afterwards I went with Salka to her place. She wants to pay next week but cannot. I threatened her with complaints. She cheats. Mrs. Matschuga promised to pay with oranges. She does not earn much selling fruit.

You will be annoyed but you should be pleased that the bed frame, even though it's broken and was left with the things to be thrown out, brought Fritz 3 marks for a chicken coop.

[This letter has writing on the side and on the top, upside down.]

[Sideways] Dear Fanny, I'm just at Lina's and read your letter. We are happy that you have now arrived. I received your card. We will write [?] together so you know everything. Send greetings on my behalf and from Irma to Walter and the children.

Your cousin Ida

———

Lina writes this second letter two years later. Note that she uses the obligatory "Sara" to sign her name.

———

From Lina (Helene Weiss) to her sister-in-law Fanny Lustig

3 January 1939, Gleiwitz

My dear Fanny,

Since I came back from [. . .] I have written you 3 letters and wonder very much that you have received so few. Maybe they will arrive sometime. I hope that all of you are enjoying good health and that your cold is gone. We are all still well, you understand me; I can't make up my mind whether to go to Georg. Perhaps if I were younger—in the last weeks I have aged 10 years; can't sleep at all without sleeping pills.

My son Alfred was away for 5 weeks and came back terribly down. That was what those who were not away did not need. Alfred's boys will probably go to Australia. Ilse [Alfred's wife?] is supposed to go to New York but it takes a long time. Yesterday Heinz Karliner and wife, [the] Adlers, [Mivdonemiks], and Günter Markus left. Niece [O . . .]velt flew to Australia. The boys [children of Margot Lustig Berger and Kurt Berger] are going to England, and so one after the other emigrates. There are no more Jewish businesses. There are also no more Jewish newspapers. Did you receive the cloth? Salka told me she had written you. You will also have received a letter from Lucie. I cannot allow myself to think about when Tommy and Lucie leave.

Sister Klara is not well at all, now has pain in the arm. I wrote you that she had to have a breast removed; the poor thing is suffering a great deal. Paula [her daughter] is supposed to [go] to Buenos Aires. What will happen? The pension is much less. Here in the home nobody gets their pension any more. Willi has not been able to receive a pass [an internal travel document] for a long time. Frenkels send you special greetings. All the other acquaintances as well. Greet and kiss the beloved children, Erna, Walter

from your true sister-in-law Lina Sara Weiss

———

Lina writes her last letter just a month later.

———

From Lina (Helene Weiss) to her sister-in-law Fanny Lustig

6 February 1939, Gleiwitz

My dear Fanny!

I don't want to make you wait any longer for my detailed letter, even though I am quite weak. In the meantime you will have received my card in which I thank you and dear Erna for the congratulations and best wishes you sent me for my 75th birthday. Sad to say it always turns out in other ways. I was in bed for 4 weeks with a very painful bladder infection. I am better today but still cannot go out, but enough of that. Our sister Klara is not well. The pain in her arm is much more noticeable . . . [It] may come from the regenerated breast and the poor thing suffers a great deal. And on top of this, she is now alone because on December 30th [her daughter] Paula left for Buenos Aires. She has a Jewish lady living with her, but she is even [. . .]. In her last letter she asked me or Lucie to come to her, but in my state of health, I cannot be asked to make such a trip. Maybe Lucie will go to her at the end of the week.

When she was here at our place last year, we tried to convince her to sell the furniture and give up the house and move into a retirement home; sadly she has not done anything. The pension that she was supposed to get from the state has certainly been reduced. Isn't dear Max [her husband] lucky that he did not live to see this?

And imagine the bad luck, the Rosenfeldts moved from England to Holland, where Samson [was] stricken and died during his operation. Klara always wanted to join them, but in her condition it was not possible. It is really sad. She will be 78 on the 8th of this month; who would have thought that during her old age she would live like this. Our brother-in-law Schroeder is always the same. He sold the house in Ramisch, but he does not yet have a permission that everyone must have, and under the military he will have very little left to live on. Let K. B. [Kurt Berger] explain this to you. Bianka is the same. Jews must sell everything.

You have no idea, dear Fanny. Here in the home it is not nice any more. In the three double rooms, where two ladies or two gentlemen were, there are now 4 people and they are the ones who no longer receive their pensions, so that those who can pay can be lodged in the rooms that have been emptied. The Rosenthals have been here since January 1; they don't have a big room, which they'd like. Then comes Mrs. Neulaender, born Spiegel, Mrs. Goldberg, Mr. Friedlaender von [B . . . obel]; the demand is very big. First most Jews must leave their homes, and then the children who are emigrating want lodging for their parents.

You, dear Fanny, can thank dear God that you are out and so well kept at your children's. You asked me if [my son] Alfred had a job. That is quite impossible, and how it will be with him I don't know. He would like the boys and Ilse to emigrate. Georg has requested an affidavit for Ilse but it takes a long time. She wants to be a maid in New York. Rudy is supposed to take 30 children to Australia, but when? Everywhere is blocked.

Bills [Wilhelm Lustig, a nephew] is working very hard so that Fanny and Luise can get to [Argentina]. And then I will be alone, I cannot even think about it. Yes, dear Fanny, for that I have grown old, to have such grief. Georg writes me but cannot send me anything. Last week Bertel left with the children for Cuba; Bianka accompanied them all the way to Hamburg. Two days before their departure, the boy had to have his eardrum pierced. He had an infection in his middle ear, so you can imagine with what feelings they traveled. In Hamburg he was already better. Your friend U. Lustig is going to Brazil shortly; his job at the [G] office is being taken over by Harweg Badrian. As long as the Jewish teachers are still here, they teach the Jewish children in the former Adler premises.

[Letter is resumed the following day.] Yesterday was Mrs. Goldstein's 80th birthday. She was very much honored. Judge (Justizrat) gave a very nice speech. She refused all presents and only wanted money so she could distribute it amongst the poor. It brought her some [. . .] and the community handed over 50 marks, so she had almost 200 marks altogether. Today is the wedding of Mrs. Printer, born Neulaender, with Mr. Paul Guttman [from] Beuthen. They are emigrating. If I would give you all the names of those who are emigrating, I would have no more room left [on the page] to write you. Did you get the keys and the cloth? Hopefully you have already received your things. Fritz Wechsberg is going to great pains to leave but nothing is working.

Kurt B. [Berger] gushed about Walter's business and about the little house where you live, and also about the children. He also writes that you, dear Fanny, look very well. The picture shows that as well. Everyone I show it to says you look 20 years younger. The [S . . .] are also cute. I would like to have seen them.

If you would see the mounds of rubble close to us, you would cry, and we have to see it every day. Now I close, I am too tired. Greet all, all your dear ones. Kurt B. I would like to greet particularly, greetings and kisses for you, your good sister-in-law, Lina [Top of page, upside down.] Fritz and Salka wrote you recently. Jenka has given her news. The 10 marks I give you happily; nothing has been said to me yet.

———

Letters from others add to the picture of Gleiwitz during this period. Kurt Berger's wife Margot—Fanny Lustig's niece—pens the following letter, the only document that specifically mentions Walter's role in helping the family. At the time, she was waiting alone in Gleiwitz, getting her last documents in order. Margot is very clear. She is forever grateful, for she is one of the six members of the Lustig family who succeeded in emigrating to Peru. Walter helped her immediate family, her husband and two sons, as well as her parents. Her husband is in Lima working for Neisser and Co., and her two sons are in England. They had left Germany on the Kindertransport, also called RCM or Refugee Children's Movement, one of the most heroic ventures of the Second World War. Between December 1938 and the beginning of the war in September 1939, nearly 10,000 predominantly Jewish children from Germany, Austria, Czechoslovakia, Poland, and the Free City of Danzig were sent to the United Kingdom, where they were placed in British foster homes, hostels, and farms for the entire war. The great majority never saw their parents again. Lutz and Ernst Berger were very fortunate because their parents were waiting for them in Lima. They were ten and fifteen years old when they left Germany and fifteen and twenty when they were reunited with their parents.

———

From Margot (Lustig) Berger to her aunt, Fanny Lustig

Early 1939, Gleiwitz

My dear good Aunt Fanny,

This year you will celebrate my [March 19] and your birthday [March 20] with my good Kurt. You will think about me, I will think about you, especially on these days. I congratulate you, dear aunt, with all my heart on your birthday. I wish that our dear God may keep you in good health for numberless years, and that you are surrounded by so much love from your loved ones, [and that?] you should live to see many beautiful and good things. "Señora Omi lebe hoch" [Dear Grandma, be blessed, be honored]. You will no doubt eat good cake in the Upper Silesian style and think about those whom you know are still here. I am always glad when Kurt writes me about you and your dear ones. The same can be said about you, my dear ones. I can do nothing else but keep telling you how grateful I am to you, and when I hear from Kurt I understand what goodness, wellbeing, and love for your closest means. There are things that one has in the innermost being that words cannot express. If I could shake your hand, you would understand. How I am doing you know since you hear it from Kurt regularly. Don't I write punctually? Today I have glued a large variety of stamps [on the envelope] for you, dear Walter. The envelopes are a little small and not many fit. Do you have specific stamps you would like? So I will close with hearty greetings for all of you. For you, dear aunt, a happy birthday kiss from your good grateful niece,

Margot

Margot's son, Lutz Berger, in response to my request to recall his child-hood experiences, wrote the following curt answer in 2012: "Both of us went by boat to London where we were received by two English families that took us to Liverpool where we stayed until the Second World War ended. Then, via the first boat that left for South America, we arrived at the port of Callao in Peru on October 22, 1945."

The Berger family soon after they were reunited. Margot stands on the right, between her husband and her son Lutz. The older man in the picture is Max Lustig, Margot's father, brother of Fanny's husband, the late Salomon. Walter's wife Erna is at the far left and daughter Helen in the center. Lima, 1946 or 1947.

Angela, Erna's non-Jewish friend, expresses a very different point of view about the situation in Germany in general and Fanny's departure in particular. Her phrase, "We must remain silent," is telling. And although Erna has already been gone for eight years, she writes about the many people they have in common. Erna and Angela most probably studied music together and shared a passion for music. While Erna remained an amateur, Angela became a professional musician, singer, and teacher, and in this letter she tells Erna about her students and upcoming performances. Noteworthy is the intimate tone and her innocent remark about visiting someone in Chicago. In our wonderful wedding picture, Angela is seated directly behind the bride. In yet another nickname twist, Angela refers to Walter as Burel or Burrel. In French *burel* is a boy with reddish brownish hair, an accurate description of Walter's hair color, and in Spanish *burrel* is an adult male bull. I obviously refuse to speculate.

From Angela Schymiczek to Erna (Lustig) Neisser, who is on her way to New York to meet Walter returning from Germany

10 January 1938, Gleiwitz

My dear Erna,

I have just received your kind letter [written] from the Grace Line and am delighted and thank you warmly for it. In my mind I can watch your travel through the Panama Canal, as Burel's film was still strong in my memory. Now you will already be stepping on New York pavement together, you will have celebrated a glorious reunion, and Erna will again be in her element and make herself beautiful and let herself be taken out and pampered. . . .

Imagine, at the end of the year I received a lovely letter from Dr. Felber in Vienna. In puncto. My connection with him was musicology. He also writes nicely about you, about when you applied [for his class?]. Elsie Hensel was here in the last year, I surely wrote you. But [. . .] she went back to Chicago. If you could meet, that would be lovely. Elsie could tell you about the lovely hours we spent, also about Prague. Her address is Chicago, Illinois, 4754 S. Wood Street.

Our friendship, our common spiritual, unforgettable journeys and beautiful [. . .]. That was a great time!

As I understand from your lines, your dear mother has landed well. That is the best solution. We have to remain silent, but you know that I always have the deepest interest in your destiny. Your dear mother will also come to love and become familiar with your home there and the grandchildren will revive her, perk her up; the small chores will give her life a purpose again. You are cared for by [Burel], therefore happy and content.

If you think of me at times, I am exceedingly pleased. I really need to go "forward," unbending, with my many skills, my patience, to find joy in work as a way to cope with life. I don't need to tell you much; you know how it was and so it goes on. I have not taken any big trips for the last two years. This year I bought myself a very nice black fur coat, with a wide collar made of silver-fox-colored Australian possum. On 6 [of February I am in Berlin, singing at the] German-Ital. Society—Kurfürstendamm Uhlandstr. 171/72 with Kapellmeistr. Comicich; then I'll be accompanying Prof. Alyss Greiner at the Academy, while she teaches her 16 students. As well, I'll join the 2 directors, L'Arnals and Prof. Niedecken-Gebhardt, in dramatic lessons. I hope for an interesting time! Ms. Ritter wrote me from Cape Town "air mail" to John Schueller. Schueller you will surely remember; he's now General Director of the State Opera of Berlin. I'll look him up. But I have little hope, because once they have made it, they get on their high horse. God, I have a modest existence, don't need his instruction. We can't take more than 4 planks with us [reference to coffin].

Carl Liboschik has developed beautifully; he sings in all the states with the police band and does me honor. I still have nice music evenings. With Ulla Warlo I diligently make music. The Dr. with his 4 boys is still available! Lilly from Nauheim is presently visiting; she helps Rudi Warlo, the able cardiac diagnostician there, and he is still single. Bon viveur!!

Otherwise everything else in our family is the same. We only want to stay healthy, have work and be able to work. Isidor Stebel, [who lived at] Ratibor St., 34 years old, committed suicide. For sure the siblings have squandered the parents' two houses and the business . . . With our friends K it looks sad. Mother Ida came back from Bozen [Bolzano] with tuberculosis. Like a shadow. So Father Franz immediately sent her back to Italy. Apparently her health is now better. This good person has already been through an awful lot. Dante is in Addis Ababa. Be well, my dear. I also wish, on behalf of my dear mother and relatives, for you and Burel a very healthy and blessed 1938, happiness and joy. With heartfelt greetings from all of us to all of you,

your good and trusted Angela

―――

We have additional letters from various members of the Lustig family.

―――

From cousin Ida [Neumann?] to Fanny Lustig

29 December 1937

My dear Fanny,

Thank you so much for the card from Buenaventura. The inhabitants of the island look quite modern, and the card was admired everywhere; even lawyer Schlesinger, whom I met at Aunt Neumark's, took the card so his children could see it. Above all, we are delighted you withstood the voyage well and have landed safely in Lima. I can imagine the joy of dear Erna and the childen and would have liked to have been present to see how it rained kisses . . . . Is Christmas celebrated there too? Well, here it is so modern that most of the Jewish people baked and ate carp. I did not tolerate much since I was not well . . . . Dear Erna should send me a new picture of the children, one where she appears. Erna will have received Fritz's letter and it would be nice if she would take some interest in him. She knows he is a rascal. . . . Maybe she can do something for him. Walter brought over his people. . . .

From Clara Lustig to her cousin Erna (Lustig) Neisser

9 January 1938

Dear Erna!

. . . Greetings to your husband. He won't have much to tell you about us since he did not spend much time with us. His family sense was not filled with the in-laws, which you can understand . . . Your mother is surprised to hear so seldom from Aunt Lina. Well, our aunt probably never liked to write; she thinks that if your mother gets the community newsletter regularly, she is well informed.

From Else (Lustig) Sack [sister of Fritz Lustig, who is mentioned in cousin Ida's letter of December 29, 1937] to her cousin Erna (Lustig) Neisser

1 February 1940, Berlin

My dear Erna,

It is almost one year since I last wrote you, but sadly I have not received an answer from you. Of course, all are busy fighting for their own problems, but I think, for me, I had the right to consider that we understood each other well and you were always a dear relative to me. For this reason, I have been saddened, dear Erna, not to have heard from you. When I asked the Gleiwitz relatives about you, especially about your dear mother, the answer was always quite sparse. In any case, let me hope that your dear family and your dear mother are well and that above all, are in good health. So much has happened during the time since we last saw each other! One does not know where to begin. That dear Moritz and I are not outside [Germany] you can see. We are now the only relatives left and at this time are sad because it is impossible for us to leave. Our Walter [her son] left for Haliborg [?] in Sweden a year ago tomorrow.

Thank God they managed to make it through. That is, he has found a good job in his field and has found dear Paula [his wife] a position in a household. She's there since June '39 where she works in an Aryan household and she is quite well so far except for the terrible homesickness and being separated from us. Although the people are very good and she is often with Walter, it is very difficult for her to overcome her homesickness. It was all planned that in October or November at the latest we would also go there.

Then came the war and buried our hopes. It is terrible for us, a great pain but we cannot change anything. On the 12/31/38 we had to give up our thriving locksmith shop and what that meant for my dear husband I need not tell you, dear Erna. Now Moritz works as an employee at a previous acquaintance and has had to accept his fate even in this. In May last year Fritz [Lustig] and Mally [his wife] emigrated to Shanghai. Heinz [their son] with his young wife had already left for there a few months before. Unfortunately, they are doing very, very badly. Fritz could not find a job and Mally is very ill. They write me that Mally should be operated but they have no money for that.

Each letter is full of yammering [complaints] so I am very unhappy because I cannot help them. Well dear Ernele, I have a big request:

Help the Lustigs. Even if it is only a small allowance. You can surely spare a few dollars once in a while. You are surely a good person. Please do me the favor of helping Fritz as much as you possibly can. You know, they did not act as well as they should have toward their sister, but in this case one cannot repay / compare the two. I hope dear Erna that I am not appealing without [_____] on your well-known generosity and do what you can do to help them. They live in such a primitive and needy way that it pains me to think about it. By the way, Berta and her friend, Mr. Schabel, are there as well. And they too have no work. You also know Hilde, wife of [_____], now Mrs. Klug. She is in Shanghai. Fritz did not want to go there but he had no other alternatives.

Now dear Erna, I want to hear about your dear family. How is your dear husband? The children must be big little people already and bring you much joy. What is the "Baby" doing? Is she still so cute? How is your mother? And also you, my dear child, I hope you are well. I would like to have answers to all these questions from you. I learned from Aunt Bianca that Margot and her dear ones are also in Lima. How are they, what are they doing? Do you have news from Gertrud in Buenos Aires? Our family is scattered all over the world! What will be our fate! By the way, is Mrs. Hirsch, Aunt Thea, still with you? Do you sometimes still remember the beautiful days in Berlin? How carefree we were and how much sadness one has been through in the meantime. I would like to have written Rudy Lustig about Fritz, but first, I do not know his address, and then he does not know me.

We often get together with Hanne (?) Fleischer. When it is possible, I invite her to come to us. She is also not well. At present, she works in a household that has 2 old ladies. At the moment it is bitterly cold here. I have rented my front room to a couple, for now the apartment was too big for us and the rent too expensive. In November, we had our silver wedding anniversary. How we felt that our nearest and dearest, especially our good son, could not be there. Walter really is a brave good boy and Paula always writes you can be proud of your son. At Christmas, it was possible to send a package. We got a fine goose and a few pounds of butter. Before he used to supply us well but now Sweden [allows] no exports. Do you know, dear Erna, I would like to be invited to your [place] for a good cup of coffee like your mother used to brew. Yes these are just unfulfillable dreams. You would make me very happy if you could soon tell me about everything in detail but I ask you again to help Fritz. Please send greetings to the Berger family, your dear Mother, your dear husband and your children, [and] very special greetings and kisses to you from

your cousin Else

[Horizontal] Fritz Lustig Ad. Friedrich Lustig, P.O. Box 1031 Shanghai (China)

———

Another cousin, Fritz Ehrlich, writes Fanny in August 1939 and March 1940.

———

From Fritz Ehrlich to his cousin Fanny Lustig

29 August 1939, Gleiwitz

My dear Fanny,

. . . Salka has gone out to the cemetery often and always visited your graves. Many have died here. Fritz W. is still here. Rosel and Lionna still get the pension. Wehrtsbergs have moved and are living very well. W. from 17 is already gone.

Schroeder and Klara Weiss are also dead but Fanny Glaser and Lina Weiss must have already written you. Paula and Fanny cannot come here at all.

Have you bought yourself a nice little dog like your Prinz? Did Erna get the books? I drove them from here to Hindenburg. Dear Fanny write us again, and hopefully you'll stay healthy for that is the main thing. We now have a small income and lack money because we are older and can't afford anything and have no help from anywhere. I myself do not know how it will be and to whom we will turn next. So dear Fanny nothing else new for today, and hopefully you will write us again soon and wish you health and all the best. Greetings to Erna and children and to Mr. Neisser. Ida will write you. With many greetings from Salka and me,

I remain your cousin Fritz Ehrlich

Regards from Lionna and Rosel Ehrlich

[Postscript from one of the many people called Fritz, whose surname and relationship are unknown.] Dear Fanny, You inquired about me and I am glad that you are still thinking of me. Unfortunately, I'm still here and no one will help me get out. Your sister Jenny [and I?] write each other from time to time. As for the meadow, it has now gone so far that it can be sold. Adolf wrote to me once from Vienna but that's already half a year ago. Jenny wants to give me something to emigrate in case the meadow is sold; I have earned nothing since November '38. What will become of us, heaven knows. Many greetings to all of you,

Fritz

From Fritz Ehrlich to his cousin Fanny Lustig

14 March 1940, Gleiwitz

. . . Dear Fanny,

We have applied to emigrate to Palestine; we have had to fill out forms where we had to specify the relatives and acquaintances who are abroad. In case there would be an inquiry, please do not forget us and the same for the Neissers. . . .

⸻

The last letter from this period is from Lima, from Fanny herself, writing from Peru to Germany. Once the war started, all correspondence ended, and the letter was either returned to the sender or is a copy Fanny made for herself. Fanny mentions both a Lina and another Fanny, but there were several in the family, so we don't know to whom she is referring. The tone is very different from my own childhood memories of an old lady who bustled around the kitchen in Lima, shooing away the children. Her permanent frown never mirrored her name Lustig, which means "funny."

⸻

From Fanny Lustig to her sister-in-law Lina (Helene Weiss)

31 March 1940, Lima

My dear Lina!

I hope that the birthday airmail letter that I sent to dear Fanny arrived in time; I also added a few lines for dear Lina. In it I also added my hearty thanks for the good wishes sent to me. I hope dear

Fanny had a good birthday. My birthday was spent very pleasantly with coffee and good cake, and I thought of you, dear Lina. I would have liked [to have] all of you as guests; the table was prepared for many guests. My children and grandchildren were the first to congratulate [me]. All three [grandchildren] recited poems; they thanked me for the love and care from early morning until late evening. Everyone gave me a gift. I was very touched that day. Unfortunately, the dearest well-wisher, my dear husband, was missing. How happy he would have been here with the grandchildren. All three go to school. Helen likes it in school. They go to an English school.

Dear Walter has landed well from his trip [to Argentina]. He gave us a lot of good news about Bills [her nephew Wilhelm Lustig]. The children look very well and have grown, and Gertrud [Wilhelm's wife] and dear Bills look well. Dear Walter met many acquaintances in Buenos Aires. [He also met] good Leipziger [people from Leipzig] who were very happy to see him. Two weeks ago, dear Erna got a nice, long letter from her [cousin Gertrud]. Elsa Sack also wrote us. She asks Erna to send Fritz L. [Lustig] money. Fritz also sent a letter last week, begging Walter to send him money to get established. I asked dear Walter what should be done. He told me he had enough here. That I can imagine since so many demands are made on him here. Fritz L. could be here, if he had not lied to Walter when Walter was in Berlin. How is Willy and what does dear Alfred do? Please greet them all . . . .

━━━━━━━

It is impossible to speculate about Walter's refusal to help Fritz Lustig. He is asked to do so repeatedly, in a direct note from Fritz himself, in a request from his sister, Else Sack, in her letter of February 1, 1940, and finally by his mother-in-law in the conversation she describes in this last letter. What happened in Berlin when Fritz Lustig lied to Walter we will never know. We do know that Walter refused him help twice, both before and after the war.

Fanny at the far left talks to her grandson Rudy. Beside her Friedrich Freund with Tito and Helen, Kaethe, and Trude holding Ursula. 1940.

CHAPTER SIX

In Our House There Was Always Music

Lima, 1936–1945

KLEINE Erna's son, Miguel / Michael Liebermann, writes,

Now that I am in my late sixties, I think a lot about my grand-father [Herman Liebermann] because in the years immediately after the Second World War, he too was in his late sixties. In Lima, he sold sausages and cold cuts, salamis of many kinds that he carried in two heavy leather cases. He had arrived in Peru about ten years earlier, leaving behind a business, a life, and now he had to make a living again in a country where he did not speak the language, or know the customs, where the way of life was totally foreign to him. Cases in hand, he went to the homes of Jews throughout the city, taking buses and trolleys, walking long blocks, learning where people lived, knocking on their doors and displaying and selling his meats. How did he manage? How did he lug those cases? How did he find the right addresses without being able to ask anyone for directions? I cannot imagine it.

While the family members in Europe grappled with the effects of Nazi rule, those in Peru dealt with very different problems. The

Helen, Rudy, and Tito Neisser on a Neisser company truck.

*Walter and Erna in front of the
Lima Country Club. 1938.*

Walter surrounded by the family members he employed.

On the right, the main store on Mantas, half a block from the Plaza de Armas, in 1940s Lima.

challenges were huge at both the individual and the community level.

Employment, usually the biggest challenge for new immigrants, was never an issue for most members of our family. With very few exceptions, everyone worked for Walter. Nevertheless, work was very much an issue for other Jewish newcomers, and most struggled. People who had owned their own clothing stores started by peddling cloth; others made and sold brooms; women sewed and mended and of course did translations and gave language lessons. During her first year in Peru, my mother was a nanny for a rich Peruvian family, taking care of the children and teaching them French.

Although the majority of Jewish immigrants had been business people, there were some professionals. Only a few were able to practice. The lawyers had no chance whatsoever. Most doctors were not allowed to practice in Lima, although exceptions were made for a few specialties. Some doctors found it easier to gain admission to the profession by living in provincial towns. For example, Dr. Hans Ruhr practiced in the high Andes, in the province of Huancavelica. If coming to Lima was difficult, the provinces were unimaginable. Housing, health, and educational facilities were substandard. Other professionals had to make their living in any way possible. Eva Jacobowitz-Baer's father, a PhD in philosophy, made industrial soap and sold it himself, and Eva's husband Walter Baer, who arrived in 1938 at the age of thirteen, had to go to work immediately to help support the family.

Dentists were readily accepted and there were three in our little community. I was related through the marriages of various aunts and uncles to two of them, Dr. Liebermann and Dr. Weinstein, but we went to the third, Dr. Benjamin. Presumably he was our dentist because his wife—whom we called Tante Grete though she was not our aunt—helped my grandmother and not because he was considered the most competent dentist. Since Dr. Liebermann and Dr. Benjamin both practiced in their homes and lived in the same small courtyard, their front doors facing each other, I learned it was best if you could visit one dentist without the other one noticing. Clearly the one my father wanted to avoid was Dr. Weinstein, who supposedly would point to his patient's teeth and exclaim, "Die ganze Scheisse raus." (The whole shit comes out.) As a child I could not understand how complicated these choices were, nor the resulting acrimony.

Although most of the Jewish refugees had no connection to Peru and were there simply because their visa application had been approved, a few had been actively recruited. Theo Buchwald was invited to found the National Symphony Orchestra. A noted Viennese musician, he in turn hired other German-speaking Jewish musicians: Leopold Palm, cello; Hans Prager, viola; Hans Lewitus, clarinet; as well as Ernst Lewitus, Bronislav Mitman, Edgar Heyman and others. I knew many of them and grew up with their children. When I contacted Hans Lewitus's widow Eva to ask for details about being hired in Peru, she answered immediately.

> Dear Evita (sorry, but that's how it came out and I'm leaving it). . . .
>
> Hans's mother lived in Vienna at the time and found out that Buchwald was hiring Jews for the Peruvian Symphony Orchestra. She wrote her son in Palestine hoping that she could meet both her sons in Lima. How Mutter Lewitus knew about Buchwald, that I don't know. Maybe it was through Huberman, who hired the best Jewish musicians in Europe to form the orchestra in what was then Palestine.
>
> Hans came from Palestine, he was the clarinetist, with Farnesi, who played contrabass (not Jewish, I think the only non-Jew

who played in the Palestine Symphony), and Sally van den Berg (oboist) and one of the Odnoposoffs, who did not stay a long time. Palm was not in Palestine. And Ernst [Lewitus] came later, from Morocco, at Hans's request. I don't know how the others came.

True to their Central European roots, the musicians also played chamber music for the sheer joy of getting together. They rehearsed in each others' homes, and when they were ready, gave concerts. It was a tiny circle of friends, all German-speaking Central Europeans, the adults all recent arrivals to Peru. I remember staring at Palm's wooden leg and hoping, as only a child can, that Prager would jump. He had a weird nervous tic that made him jump straight up, viola in hand. Walter's daughter Helen also remembers the musicians:

> [In our house] there was always classical music playing, either records or on the radio. My mother sang Lieder . . . My brother Tito accompanied her on the piano. She would organize musical events at home, inviting artists of the caliber of the cellist Odnoposoff and his sister Nélida, who was a good friend. Members of the Symphony Orchestra played at these events, including musicians like Hans Lewitus, Theo Buchwald, Yolanda Kronberger, Mitman and others I don't remember.

Two Peruvian universities made notable appointments, the University of San Marcos in Lima and the University of Trujillo in northern Peru. The Dresden psychologist Walter Blumenfeld had a long and successful career at San Marcos. In his three-volume book, *I Will Bear Witness: A Diary of the Nazi Years*, Victor Klemperer often refers to Blumenfeld, who was one of his closest friends. Klemperer charts Blumenfeld's story starting with his dismissal from his university

The musical gatherings in Walter's living room were for friends, not relatives. Yet the members of our family were invited all the time; all the family events took place at his house and his generosity was extraordinary. Walter and Erna skillfully balanced several social circles and made everyone feel important. They cultivated a vast network of friends and acquaintances, including the very influential political and business elite.

position in Dresden in 1934, to the anguished decision to accept the offer in Lima, through the payment of the 25 percent Reich Flight Property Tax and the letters in which Blumenfeld wrote that he and his wife felt like exiles in Peru.

Dr. Hans Horkheimer arrived in Trujillo in 1939. A pioneer in Peruvian archeology, he is credited with several great finds, including Chancay and Huaral, as well as the first comprehensive list of the cultures of the coast. Horkheimer, nicknamed Horki, visited us frequently, and my mother, who became very interested in Peruvian archeology, would go out to the digs with him. For his friends in the German-speaking Jewish community, he organized tours of the sites within easy driving distance from Lima. Ruth Shine remembers that several cars would meet at an appointed place on a Sunday morning, everyone with picnic baskets filled. Horkheimer would go in the lead car and it was always an honor to take him. Once on the site he would guide the group, explaining in such a manner that his audience could understand, mixing humor and great knowledge, while his audience listened and took pictures. These outings were entirely in German.

Learning Spanish presented another great challenge for the refugees. Everyone needed Spanish for work, but at home all the adults spoke German, although the children usually answered in Spanish. In Peru there was no societal pressure to speak Spanish, nor was there any anti-German feeling, so speaking German on the street was never an issue. Walter, his brother, sisters, and in-laws spoke only German to each other. Miguel Liebermann specifically requested I include the Neisser and Nothmann standard greeting. One sibling would exclaim: "Erich Neisser, Hosen scheisser" (pants shitter), and the answer would be "Erna Neisser, Hosen scheisser" followed by laughter and the admonition by someone else to watch their language.

My father was adamant about the language spoken in our house. It was German and only German, and if I answered in Spanish, his stock answer was "Ich verstehe nicht" (I don't understand). It was obvious to both of us that he understood perfectly well, but he felt languages were a great asset, and the more languages one spoke the better. He maintained this attitude with all of his nephews and nieces and with my friends. He was such a gentle person that nobody really minded and some of my friends whose parents were not strict about language have told me that they were grateful he had insisted on speaking only German.

Spanish proficiency varied according to the generation. Those of us born in Peru were native speakers. Spanish was the language of the street and some of our schooling. For our parents, it was the language of work; and for the grandparents' generation, it simply did not happen. Among the adults the degree of correct Spanish usage and pronunciation varied a great deal. Some, even after twenty years in Peru, sounded as if they had just arrived; others could pass for native speakers. The most extreme cases were my father, who never mastered Spanish pronunciation, and sister Kaethe's husband, Willy Simenauer, whose Spanish was impeccable. Walter's Spanish was excellent but slightly accented.

The grandparents' generation never learned Spanish. Fanny Lustig, Walter's mother-in-law, lived with Walter and his family and spent her days in the kitchen, where she took charge of food preparation. Helen remembers, "Sauerbraten, gefuellte Fisch, Sauerkraut, Rouladen, Streuselkuchen, Barchis, Apfelstrudel, Mohnkuchen." Fanny spoke German, and her trademark phrase "No boino," meaning not good, is incorrect in both Spanish and German. Pancha, the maid who started working in the house as a young woman and spent the next forty years with the family, spoke only Spanish. How they communicated is a mystery. Eleven years after her arrival in Peru, Fanny writes her grandson Rudy who has been sent away to boarding school. The postscript from Pancha, the maid, is in Spanish.

———

From Fanny (Lanzer) Lustig to Rudy Neisser at boarding school in Massachusetts

24 May 1949

My dear Rudy,

Thank you dear Rudy for your nice letter but I am not satisfied because you write me in Spanish and I cannot read it yet. I'm not blaming you, but I'm sorry that you cannot write in German.

Well, my dear Rudy, for your birthday my warmest congratulations and my desire that you remain healthy and bring your dear parents much joy. I cannot send you a birthday present, but I promise that when you come back again to visit, you'll get a late birthday cake. I also wanted to enclose chocolate with the books I sent, but Uncle Erich said it was not allowed. As for my health, I'm well, thank God. I cannot work nor go to pray. I still go to the doctor, and have to be carried down the stairs. I have to lie down a great deal.

Do you have any news from your parents [who are visiting the new state of Israel]? I have had no news from Tel Aviv. How are dear Helen and dear Tito? Please send them warm regards from me. Do you live far from Helen?

Have an enjoyable and pleasant birthday. Be warmly greeted and kissed by

your good Omi Lustig

The staff also sends their regards to you. [?] and [?] send congratulations as well. Pancha's son Carlos congratulates you for your birthday. [Postscript in Spanish from Pancha, the maid] Rudy, I'd also like to wish you a happy birthday on the 27th. Please send greetings from me to Tito.

Pancha

═══════════

Whereas Walter integrated into the Peruvian world, the rest of the family did not. Clearly Walter was an immigrant; he had left Germany in 1923 to seek his fortune in the New World. It was his choice and a decision he embraced. His three sisters, their spouses, his brother, and his mother were refugees, and when they arrived in Peru in the late 1930s, getting out of Germany was a priority for them. They were all too aware that many of those left behind desperately sought visas to any country that would accept them. They were grateful to have escaped Nazi Germany, grateful for the reconstitution of the family in Lima, and grateful for the work possibilities offered. But would they have left their home country if circumstances had been different? Perhaps, as it became obvious that Walter was now prosperous, some might have left, but certainly not all. One of the most telling facts is that there were so few children. Many members of the Neisser family had an only child, and among the Nothmanns many opted for not having any. Walter's Nothmann cousins, Tilde Nothmann, Henny Nothmann, Erna Nothmann, Kaethe Nothmann—all married women of childbearing age—remained childless. Only Walter and Erna had three children.

Whereas Walter had friends and was integrated to a certain extent into the Peruvian elite, his siblings recreated, as best they could, the world they had left. Marginalized by cultural barriers, language, and religion, they lived within their own circle. My father's best friend was his cousin Guenter Nothmann; cousin Ruth visited Kleine Erna almost every day; the Neisser brothers and sisters gathered at their mother's on Friday nights; and the entire family met at one of Walter's houses almost every Sunday. Being a refugee carries baggage of loss, homesickness, longing for a world the person has been forced to flee. Not only were the Neisser siblings living in an alien world, but they were also overwhelmed by the knowledge that so many friends and family could not escape.

Along with their fellow Jewish refugees, the members of the Neisser and Nothmann families worked actively to help the new arrivals. The Peruvian Jewish community numbered barely 2,500 people and the great majority were still facing huge challenges as they tried to get their own lives in order, but starting in 1935 the work they did to settle and integrate those getting off the boats was extraordinary. Fortunately the community aid was such that within months of their arrival, the Jewish refugees were already helping the next group find work and somehow get settled.

In 1935, in order to deal with the steady flow of refugees, the three Jewish communities in Lima joined to form a Jewish Immigrant Protection Committee (Comité de Protección de los inmigrantes israelitas). As the need grew, a special fund was established to rent a house with space for about thirty people to stay until they could find their own accommodations. Every refugee received a monthly subsidy for Spanish lessons and rent. The local community raised some money, and the JOINT—the American Joint Distribution Committee, the New York-based Jewish relief organization—sent additional funds. However, in December 1939 the JOINT decided to stop sending funds to Peru. Because of the deteriorating situation in Poland, all funds were going to save Polish Jews. The local Jewish Immigrant Protection Committee would have to raise its own money. Clearly there was a lot of work to be done.

Two volunteers from the community met each arriving boat. March 1939 was the busiest month, when nine boats docked. The volunteers had no prior information about how many people would disembark in Lima's port of Callao. Some refugees held visas for Chile and Argentina, but the great majority went on to Bolivia, where visas were easier to obtain. The volunteers did whatever was necessary, greasing palms and dealing with the local authorities.

In the early war years, 1940 and 1941, the Peruvian government refused to accept further refugees although there were always individual exceptions. The last passenger vessels from Europe made it to Cuba, but then both the boats and the postal service ceased. Like most Latin American countries, Peru remained neutral in the early war years—until the government signed a series of commercial treaties with the United States in order to receive military aid. Then it effectively took sides in the conflict. In 1942, Peru, along with its fellow Latin American states, broke diplomatic relations with Germany and Vichy France. Nazi propaganda was prohibited, and within months the vast majority of German and Japanese citizens were unfairly and cruelly deported from Peru to internment camps in Mexico and the United States.

Nevertheless, boats arrived from Japan carrying Jewish refugees who had crossed Asia, landed in Japan, and found a freighter to transport them across the Pacific. Between November 1940 and January 1941, four Japanese ships with refugees on board arrived in Peru. Just like in the late 1930s when the refugees came from Europe, the local volunteers did their utmost to manage the paperwork to allow them to disembark. But it was much more difficult.

According to Thomas Connell, who describes the whole sad story in *America's Japanese Hostages*, the first ship, the *Rakuyo Maru*, carried fifty refugees who wanted to disembark either in Ecuador, where the boat was supposed to stop first, or in Peru, its second stop. A series of cables flew across the Pacific requesting steep payments despite the fact they had already been made. The Japanese wanted $400 US per family plus an additional $100 for the return trip should the passengers be refused entry. In some cases, the passenger's specific port of disembarkation was not stated. For the Jewish refugee committees working in Quito and Lima as well as the JOINT in New York, it was a bureaucratic nightmare. Even though each case had to be solved separately, nobody was sent back to Japan.

The second ship, the *Ginyo Maru*, left Japan in October 1940. The refugees held visas for Peru (one), Guatemala (one), Paraguay (one), Brazil (one), Bolivia (eleven), and Ecuador via Peru (fifteen). An additional fourteen people carried visas for the United States but it was not clear when they would be able to travel to and enter that country. In Panama City, officials requested $22,200 US to allow the fourteen to disembark. When that amount could not be raised, the ship sailed southward, and the Ecuadorian and Peruvian refugee committees hurried to obtain ninety-day permits for the passengers. A payment of $100 US per person enabled them to disembark in Ecuador on January 18, 1941, and they traveled to their final destination in the US from there.

The third ship, the *Heiyu Maru*, stopped first in Los Angeles on October 22, 1940, then headed south to various South American ports. Jewish refugees disembarked in Mexico, Colombia, Ecuador, and Peru. Once they reached southern Peru, the vast majority, forty-five people going to Bolivia, had no problem disembarking. Nevertheless, the eight with visas for Chile were denied entry and had to stay on board and travel north all the way to Mexico before the local Jewish refugee protection committees could organize the documents necessary to prevent them from being returned to Japan. In addition, typhoid fever broke out on board and two refugees perished.

The fourth ship, the *Hie Maru*, left Kobe in November 1940 and docked first in Los Angeles, where 100 of the 190 refugees disembarked. But at the next port of call, the Panamanians again refused thirty-two people scheduled to go from Panama to Costa Rica, Haiti, Brazil, Argentina, or Ecuador, allegedly because their visas had expired during the passage. The Jewish refugee protection committees in Ecuador and Peru finally succeeded in obtaining visas for some passengers to disembark in Callao, but the port authorities rejected those crossing to Argentina and Brazil, who needed transit visas. Only a few refugees were allowed to disembark. The ship continued south with full knowledge that the most difficult port, Valparaiso, which regularly refused refugees, would prove impossible. At the last port of call, there were still eighteen people on board. As the *Hie Maru* headed back to Ecuador, the Ecuadorian authorities demanded a deposit of $500 per family plus a payment of $100 for every individual for a total of $5,600 US to allow the eighteen refugees to disembark. It was only through the timely intervention of the German-Jewish mining baron, Dr. Moritz (Don Mauricio) Hochschild in Bolivia, that this huge amount was raised and the refugees were allowed to stay.

Lima's Jewish Immigrant Protection Committee ceaselessly pressured the government to accept more refugees. Probably the strangest initiative was their 1938 request to permit 1,000 refugees to enter the country to establish an agricultural colony modeled on colonies established in Argentina under the auspices of the Baron de Hirsch and in Bolivia under Mauricio Hochschild. Walter headed the list of community representatives even though the German Jews made up only 20 percent of the community. The community was willing to transport the refugees to their destination, provide lodging and agricultural machinery, and guarantee that the newcomers would stay in the settlement area. Their generosity was extraordinary and speaks to the palpable fear about events in Germany. But in the end their petition was denied.

The war years were difficult, and living in Peru presented strange problems, some related to the big picture, others very local. The terrible earthquake of 1940 destroyed large parts of Lima. Walter documented the damage only a few kilometers from his house.

Walter's photo of earthquake damage in Lima. 1940.

Another shock, albeit of a very different kind, came when German Jews were deprived of their German citizenship, rendering them stateless. The Peruvian Ministry of the Exterior recorded this information: "On the 21st of August, 1942, Erich Neisser, born in Gleiwitz June 25, 1899, with German passport number 818, issued in Beuthen on July 17th, 1933, was requested by the German Embassy in Lima to renounce his nationality." Being stateless meant they could be deported at any time, adding considerably to their insecurity. The Peruvian state also made it clear that Jews had little possibility of naturalization. As the historian Milagros Martínez-Flener writes, "Sadly, in those years Peru had an anti-Semitic policy."

Carrying only the compulsory Foreigners Card (Carnet de Extranjería) further underlined the distance from mainstream Peruvian society that family members felt. They perceived that they were not well regarded, and they did not socialize with the locals. Again Walter was the exception. Having obtained his Peruvian citizenship in the 1930s, he held a privileged position, knew ministers, and was invited to presidential gatherings.

Nevertheless, the Neisser and Nothmann families prospered and grew. Some members who had arrived childless or who had recently married decided to have children.

Walter's mother, Martha, holding two grandchildren born in 1942, myself on the left, Miguel Liebermann on the right.

By 1942, Neisser and Co. had several divisions, and members of the family worked in all of them. Kaethe and her husband owned Neisser Regalos; cousin Guenter Nothmann ran the heavy

Helen, Eva, Vera, and Ursula.

Walter, Eva, and Martha.

machinery division, Neisser Maquinaria, later called Metalum; niece Ruth Angress was the general sales manager; Kleine Erna's husband Heinz managed the Callao store; cousins Herbert, Curt, and Rudy Nothmann had management positions in the downtown offices. Two members of the Lustig family, Kurt and his son Lutz, were also integrated into the company. Walter was always its president.

Neisser and Co. continued to have a monopoly over government electrical installations for the entire country. In addition, the company represented a large number of American and European companies, including Westinghouse, Admiral, Outboard Motors International (Johnson), Kenwood, Fisker and Nielsen, and many more. It sold lamps, refrigerators, stoves, and washing machines as well as industrial kitchen supplies. More importantly, it sold machinery for both the sugar and the mining industries and measuring equipment for several other industries. There was a warehouse, a repair service, and a fleet of trucks.

The sign reads BUY ELECTRICAL MATERIALS AT NEISSER.

When Walter was ready to expand outside Lima in either 1939 or 1940 he chose Arequipa, the second biggest city in the country, and named Ulrich (Ulli) Neisser as manager. Ulli's story is unparalleled in our family. He was the first to convert and the first to join the Peruvian elite. He was the only one in his generation to fully integrate into the mainstream culture. But since he was a distant relative who lived more than 500 kilometers away, his world was of little interest to most of us.

Ulli's daughter Patricia, whom I have never met and who refers to Walter as Mr. Neisser, recounts that Walter fell ill on one of his visits to Germany. The doctor recommended to him in Breslau turned out to be a distant relative, Dr. Emil Neisser. He and Walter got along well and exchanged information about their mutual famous relative, the so-called gonorrhea Neisser, the well-known nineteenth-century physician and scientist Dr. Albert. In 1936 Dr. Emil wrote Walter asking for help for his son Ulrich, and in typical fashion, Walter came to his assistance. Once Ulrich arrived in Lima, he joined the other relatives at Neisser and Co. Two years later Dr. Emil made a second request, this time on his own behalf, as well as for his wife and his son Wolfgang. Walter again came to the rescue.

Ulrich was talented, and Walter, as usual a shrewd judge of people, sent him off to start and run the store in Arequipa. Ulrich worked for Walter for a few years, then opened his own business. In 1941 he converted to Catholicism to marry a young lady from the governing elite: The Peruvian president Óscar Benavides was one of her relatives, and her grandparents were wealthy landowners who lived in the largest mansion in Arequipa. Ulrich Neisser became a politician in his own right, twice serving as a very successful and popular mayor of Arequipa. One of his most important achievements was the creation of a savings and loan association (Asociación Mutual de Crédito y Ahorro) for which he was honored by both the Peruvian and the German governments. According to his daughter, he not only accepted German citizenship when it was returned in the early 1950s, but also carried a German diplomatic passport. Although he distanced himself from the family, his parents and brother lived in Lima and were frequent visitors at Walter's house.

Walter's house contrasted sharply with the modest rental housing where other members of the family lived. In 1937 he had bought land with Pacific Ocean views just two blocks from where the family was renting on the Malecón 28 de Julio. Walter's daughter Helen believes the house was built in 1938 and they moved in 1939.

The exterior of Walter's house in Miraflores.

The pool at Walter's house.

How can I describe Walter's house? It was probably ten times bigger than mine, with a pool, a servants' wing, and a glassed-in terrace off the living room where Walter had his breakfast. Because Rómulo, the butler, opened the front door wearing a black uniform and white gloves, we mostly came in the side entrance, beside the pool. I will describe only the library, not because I spent a lot of time there, but because it mirrored Walter. A small room on the ground floor, it was lined with back-lit bookcases enclosed by glass doors. A dark cherry-colored fabric covered the interiors. Most of the books were in German, some in English, a few in Spanish. For Walter, who read poetry, there were collections of Heine and Goethe; for Erna there were books devoted to art. The shelves also held a complete *Encyclopædia Britannica*—which prompted me to do my homework there, even though the library was much darker than the rest of the house. Walter and Erna displayed their very special colonial silver collection directly in front of the books.

Peruvian colonial silver from Walter and Erna's collection.

The library also had a secret room, one I knew nothing about until I started writing this book. If you pushed a certain spot on one of the bookcases, a door would swing forward, revealing two or three steps that led to the secret chamber. What was hidden here? Daughter Helen remembers only the bottles of liquor, locked away from her brothers. And who had the keys? Nobody remembers.

In addition to the silver collection in the library, there were several other collections: Peruvian indigenous pottery, paintings, modern silverwork, and of course Walter's large stamp collection. His stamps were probably closest to Walter's heart: He had collected them from childhood. Several family members shared his passion. Jack Nothmann writes: "I remember the many visits to the house in Miraflores and the room on the second floor where Walter always worked on his stamps." So valuable was his collection that when he traveled abroad he did not normally carry cash. Instead he brought a few select stamps that could always provide ready money.

Walter followed political events closely and continued to work on behalf of the Jewish community. After sitting on the board of La 1870 for several years, he was elected president in 1944 and served for a two-year period in a time of great turmoil. The members of La 1870 had been holding monthly meetings since 1938. First they noted the deaths in the community and observed a minute of silence; next they read and approved the minutes of the previous meeting and approved new members; then they took care of the business of the day. Finally, the high point arrived: the speaker. Every meeting had a speaker. The subjects were as varied as the members of the community and included talks on history, literature, geography, and present-day concerns. Walter was a frequent speaker. In December 1939, he reported on the JOINT's decision to stop sending funds to Peru. In 1944 he described how the organization spent its money, and in 1945 he spoke twice, first on how to give a talk and later on Peruvian public opinion. That same year he informed the assembly that he had accepted an official place on the Pro-Palestine Committee, explaining that he was not a devout Zionist, but felt a home had to be found for the Jewish people.

In November 1944, Walter became one of the 1,500 delegates from twenty-six countries that attended the World Jewish Congress War Emergency Meeting in Atlantic City. It was no accident that he was chosen. He was one of the few members of the community who could afford the trip, and because he held Peruvian citizenship, he had the legal papers necessary to travel. Upon his return, he summarized the conference's conclusions, which included a call for rehabilitation and restitutions. Six months later, in June 1945, he was charged with the painful task of announcing that lists of names of survivors from several concentration camps were available at La 1870 office.

CHAPTER SEVEN

I Hope This Wretched War Will Soon End

The Nothmann Family Letters and Memorabilia, 1941–1946

THANKS to Frank Nothmann, who kept the correspondence of his grandmother, the formidable Regina, we are fortunate to have several letters that give a first-hand account of daily life—and of our family's life in particular—in Lima during the war years. Smart and bossy, Walter's aunt Regina resided with her son Guenter and his wife Thea from 1941 to 1946. She was certainly not an easy mother-in-law, to put it mildly. She told her daughter-in-law what to do, how to do it, and when to do it, and we surmise it was this behavior that caused Regina to leave for New York in 1946, although the official explanation was that her daughter Gerda, who had no children and worked outside the home, needed her mother's help in the house. In 1961 Regina returned to Lima and spent her last years in the Jewish old people's home.

Regina was part of the Nothmann contingent that Walter helped bring to Peru—the five elderly aunts and uncles who were his mother Martha's siblings and in-laws. Accompanied by spouses and children, most of the thirty-five Nothmanns arrived between

1937 and 1941, except for the last two, Josef and Bianca, Walter's aunt and uncle, who came after the war. Only one aunt and her family perished in the Holocaust, and inexplicably, another landed in Bolivia, not Peru.

Regina, her son Guenter, and his wife Thea arrived in Lima separately. Regina's grandson Jack writes: "My father must have arrived in 1938. My mother arrived several months after my father because first the boat went to the U.S.A. where she had an emergency operation. After this she stayed with a family in Baltimore. When she arrived in Callao [Lima's port] she was not allowed to disembark because the authorities said her visa was false. She ended up in Arequipa. I believe Walter was able to get her a permit to go on to Lima."

Regina's three letters are addressed to her daughter Gerda in New York, whom she calls by the German diminutive Gerdel. Written in 1942 and 1943, they reflect the dual reality of being safe and worrying about those left behind. At that point Regina was living in Lima with her son and daughter-in-law among a vast network of family members and getting used to her new home. On the one hand, Regina describes family gatherings, birthday parties, and normal everyday events, and on the other hand she is terrified by the deafening silence from Germany. Two of her four children are safe. Guenter is in Lima, working for Walter. Gerda, who left Germany in 1938 and entered the US via Cuba, is now in New York, married, and running her own business designing and making children's clothes. But Regina has no information about her two other children and their families: her eldest son, Herbert, who was already in jail when she left Germany, her son Hans, the wives of both men, and Hans's daughter, her granddaughter.

━━━━━━━━━━

From Regina (Boehm) Nothmann to her daughter Gerda (Nothmann) Colbert and son-in-law Werner Colbert in New York

27 August 1942 [Lima]

My beloved children,

Even though I don't have a confirmation, I assume you have received [my letter]. Here time flies by like in a dream and it will soon be a year that I have been away from Europe. I experienced great joy spending Rosh Hashanah with some of my children. Unfortunately, sad memories awake in me, but I want to divert some of these sad thoughts so I can see you in my mind, my good Gerdel with your dear Werner. May you be granted a happy and healthy New Year. [My] sincerest wish is to be together with you as well some time. [I hope] you are both healthy and that your lives go in a customary way.

It is surely not easy for you; the war requires sacrifices from every single one [of us] that we gladly make. One cannot fight enough against the heaven-screaming injustices that defenseless people in Germany are exposed to. It breaks my heart when I think of Herbert, who has already sat behind prison walls for 1½ years and legally has done nothing wrong. I have no news. I did not learn of the verdict [in his case] before my departure because the date was postponed. I begged the lawyer to take care of Herbert. Unfortunately there is not much he can do for a Jew. I wrote to Hans and asked him to write Herbert. When I was still there, he was in Potsdam, where I visited him often. From there he was sent away, where I do not know. And Hans, Vera, Renate, where could they be? The poor child, how cute she always was. On September 12 she will be 6 [years old]. If only we could help these poor little arms after the war [*sic*].

Regina's daughter-in-law Vera (Friedlaender) Nothmann and granddaughter Renate.

I am getting more and more used to my new home. Unfortunately my health leaves much to be desired. The bladder infections occur too frequently and cause me excruciating pain. I think that when the summer comes it will be better. I lack warmth; we have no sun for 5 months, only rain. Because of the humid air, the rooms are so cold that I am constantly freezing. Outside it is warmer. You will certainly laugh at me. I had not imagined something like this. Thea is not always well and Guenter desperately needs some rest because of the great distance [he travels] to his work place. He comes home tired and harassed. How is Betty? Is her father there already? Please greet them warmly. You, my beloved Gerdel, and your dear Werner, all the best. I kiss you and hug you and greet you both cordially,

your good Mother

Regina and her late husband did not attend Walter and Erna's wedding, but three of her four children stand together in the wedding portrait: The handsome actor and eldest son, Herbert; the youngest and only girl, Gerda; and Guenter, who later headed one of Walter's Peruvian companies, Metalum. Missing from the wedding picture is Hans. At Walter's wedding Regina's children were still single. Ten years later, in 1940, they were all married and Hans had a little girl. Frank Nothmann comments: "It's interesting to compare the picture we have [of Herbert] with the wedding picture. We can see it is definitely Herbert. And I remember my mother told me Herbert was an actor and his stage name was Cellini."

From Regina (Boehm) Nothmann to Gerda (Nothmann) Colbert

19 January 1943 [Lima]
My dearly beloved Gerdel,

Finally after so long, again a letter from you. All kinds of thoughts come to me when I don't get a sign of life from you. Unfortunately I see that you were ill and I hope that you have recovered and all is well again. I think you spare yourself too little and work too hard. I can imagine that many demands are made on you and I know your sense of duty when

Herbert Cellini

Herbert Nothmann, Regina's eldest son.

probably too little [that you do] is recognized. The only consolation [is] that during the summer you get plenty of holiday time and can devote several weeks to your health. How much I'd like to help and relieve you of your household tasks and take care of you. I know it would be necessary. My great hope that the war will soon be over and we will see each other again sustains me. How do you really manage [your job] with the housekeeping? You probably don't eat lunch at home. Nevertheless there is plenty to do and you probably work hard at home in the evenings. In any case I wish both of you much luck in your new jobs.

I would have not believed that my letter, sent for your birthday, would take 2 months [to arrive]. I was quite annoyed about it. It is usually the case that one saves on the wrong thing. Guenter gives me 5 soles pocket money every month and most of the time he takes the letters to the post office. But although I make monthly calculations, there are always unforeseen expenditures. Last month I earned a few soles because I picked up an eight-year-old girl from school. Unfortunately there are holidays now that last until April. Since January it has been unbearably hot. One sweats like in a steam bath and is not able to do anything.

The days fly by. I have been here over 1 year and often get together with my travel companions from the ship. Every 14 days we sit comfortably, have coffee and cake, and talk about our experiences. We are 8 women and we even celebrate our birthdays. I enjoy sewing for the Red Cross. Everyone is enthusiastic about the project and much gets done. Of course Thea also participates.

On February 2 we had a big party. Aunt Martha [Walter's mother, Martha] turned 70. On the day itself and the day after, a big coffee party took place at her home. In the evening, there was a dinner in Walter's colorfully illuminated garden. All the relatives, over

40 people, arrived and it was a really successful celebration. Aunt received many gifts. Walter led the way with 500 soles. Aunt has recovered well after major surgery and is again her old self. [Kleine] Erna also looks well and is happy with her little boy, now 10 months old. I also talked to Hilde [Nothmann] Bobrowsky [Salo's daughter]; she has a good job with a Mr. See. It was the first time I saw Bobrowsky since I've been here. He is very depressed. Doesn't get together with anybody; he doesn't earn much and has to work [??]. Gerhard, their son, sides with the mother. Hilde looks pretty and young, is just a little too fat. [Hilde's sister] Kaethe is in Buenos Aires with her husband but she doesn't like it. Walter's wife was in Buenos Aires recently and Kaethe told her she very much wanted to go to Lima. [Eventually Walter helped bring the couple to Lima.] Uncle Salo probably did not make it out even though he's 72 years old and got his visa before me.

I received two reports about [my daughter-in-law, Herbert's wife] Leni through the Red Cross; the last news was from June 14th in Breslau. [My eldest son] Herbert is healthy . . . . No news from you nor from Max, Ruth, Heinz. I've written to Leni through the Red Cross. I have absolutely no news from [my second son] Hans. You can imagine how all of that depresses me. How they both must suffer only God knows and one can't help. Poor Max Koenigsberger [Leni's father] was not spared and the unfortunate Leni does not know where he is. The same with Heinz's young wife; she must have been sent to a camp somewhere. Heinz stayed in [?].

My health leaves a lot to be desired. I suffer a great deal because the gallbladder attacks occur more often and are worse. If only I could be with you, my dear child, I know I would be healthier. Stay healthy; be kissed and hugged by

your Mother

[Postscript] Dear Werner,

I was so delighted you found work in your own field; success will follow. The news about your father I read with sadness. On the one hand, you can be comforted that he is in hospital where he can be cared for. I hope and wish that he will recover there. What has become of the aunts? Have you heard from them? I feel very sorry for all those who are there. How is it possible that a single tyrant tortures and murders millions of people? There is no language to describe such a bloodhound—out of the question. Keep well and many warm greetings.

Yours, Regina

Right now it is 29 degrees [84 degrees Fahrenheit] in the shade. I've had enough and am happy to have finished writing.

*Regina in Lima.
1944.*

Regina's son can afford to give her only 5 soles in weekly pocket money, while Walter's gift to his mother is 500 soles. Obviously money is short because in her next letter Regina writes about the cost of specific food items and nylon stockings and the $10 US remittance she has just received from her daughter in New York. The second comment in her letter that bears mentioning is the baptism of Lothar Nothmann's daughter [the grandchild of Moritz]. Certainly one of the many consequences of the Holocaust was that many Jews abandoned their religion and became converts to the majority faith. They felt that the price for being Jewish was too high and did not want their children to suffer. Regina writes about the first baptism in the family and simply says that everyone disapproved.

Locating people during and after the war was very difficult. Regina writes about how friends from Germany who are living in Brazil found her through an advertisement in the *Aufbau*, a monthly newspaper that began publication in New York in the 1930s and is still in circulation, now out of Zurich. Written in English and German, it is meant specifically for German Jews around the world. Today the *Aufbau* database is online; in the 1940s, when Regina was reading it, the *Aufbau* was a valuable source of information. Starting in 1944, the newspaper printed lists of Holocaust survivors collected by different organizations and Displaced Persons camps. In addition, the newspaper ran advertisements for families and friends trying to locate their loved ones. In this case, Regina's friends, who had emigrated to Brazil, found her in Peru. Both Helen and I remember that everyone in the family subscribed and the older generation pored over the information.

From Regina (Boehm) Nothmann to Gerda and Werner

28 March 1943 [Lima]

My beloved children,

Above all things I hope you are healthy. Thank God that is also the case with us. Guenter also wanted to write but he postponed it from one day to the next. Today is Sunday and Thea and Guenter were invited for the weekend by acquaintances and I am alone in the house. Then my thoughts are always with you, and my longing to see you again, my golden [child], is great.

I hope this wretched war will soon end. What do you think, dear Werner? Your opinion always calms me. How is business? I think [it's going] well. How do you like it, Gerdel? Good results? You no doubt have a great deal of work. Is everything as expensive where you are? Prices have gone up a great deal here, and not only that, some food items are hard to get. For example, one egg costs 30 cents, one chicken 8–15 soles, a liter of milk 50 cents, 450 grams of butter 2.90. Such items were always expensive, now they are either not available or unaffordable. Nylon stockings cost between 45 and 85 soles. But otherwise life is beautiful and bearable here.

The birthdays do not end. This month especially was crazy. Yesterday I was at Curt and Tilde [Nothmann's] the whole evening (the children had already left on Saturday). It was Aunt Amanda's birthday and it was celebrated at Curt's. It is quite far for me to get there and Curt brought me home in his car. They always ask about you and send you regards. Tilde is quite plump and her only occupation is playing bridge. In general, many of the women spend their time playing bridge.

Lothar is well now. His wife had typhus and spent 6 weeks in the American hospital. The child is seven years old now, and half a year ago was baptized as a Catholic; there was great disappointment among us.

Aunt Martha is very healthy and has a beautiful house with a garden where she lives alone with a maid. Walter behaves fabulously not only with his mother but also with his siblings. He paid [the expenses] for [Kleine] Erna's illness, which cost a great deal. Walter has offered Thea a job as supervisor in the main store but she can't accept it. Thea says she could not stand all day because she has pain in her feet. However, not everything is easy in this climate. The weather is pleasant now that autumn has begun. I am still sweating enough, and later in the evening it is so cool that I shiver.

My child, do you remember the Steuer family from Berlin? I correspond with them. They had put an advertisement in the *Aufbau* to ask if I was in Lima. They wrote in such a heartfelt and happy manner that I had been able to escape and [they] ask for news about you. The Steuers are well in Rio. Hilde has a four-year-old boy. Inge is with her parents and has a good job.

On March 22 the long expected money—$10—arrived and I thank you a great deal for it. It provided much rejoicing. I took 10 soles to use for a dress I need to have redone, the rest I gave to Guenter. My acquaintances also receive money from their children that takes only 10–12 days. They get a registered airmail letter with a check for a specific bank. My dear ones, I wish you all the best. Let us hear from you soon. Gerdel,

heartfelt greetings and kisses from your loving Mother

In addition to Regina's letters, we have the correspondence of her son Hans. It is extraordinarily difficult to comment on the letters Hans (John) writes in 1945 and 1946, after four years in concentration camps and the loss of both his wife and daughter. Frank Nothmann writes: "Hans was in three concentration camps, first Theresienstadt, then three years in Auschwitz, and transferred from there to

Sachsenhausen. His wife and daughter Renate perished in Auschwitz. After being liberated from concentration camps, Hans met Dita, who became his second wife, at the Deggendorf displaced persons camp for Jewish refugees in Bavaria."

Hans Nothmann's Deggendorf Displaced Persons Center identity card. Note that his name is given as both Jan and Hans. The Czech authorities changed his name when he was first interned in Theresienstadt in 1941. The number that appears on this card, 170651, was tattooed on his forearm.

It is again almost impossible for a modern reader to grasp that having survived, Hans was transferred to a DP (Displaced Persons) Camp in the American Zone and did not know how to contact his family. He knew some relatives were in Peru, others in the United States, but of course he had no addresses. We have the remarkable first letter sent to his brother, written and mailed on his behalf by an American soldier at the camp. The envelope has no street address whatsoever and says only "Lima / Miraflores." Small miracles do happen since it landed in his brother's hands.

Letter from PFC Harry M. Schwalb in Germany to Guenter Nothmann in Lima.

Dear Mr Nothmann,

I am an American soldier stationed in Deggendorf, Bavaria. I met Hans in the camp we are now administrating. You may write to find at my address.

Sincerely,

PFC. HARRY M. SCHWALB
33696621 A-T Co. 329 INF.
APO 83, POSTMASTER, N.Y., N.Y.

Envelope without a street address sent to Guenter Nothmann.

━━━━━━━━

From PFC Harry M. Schwalb in Germany to Guenter Noth-mann in Lima

Dear Mr. Nothmann,

    I am an American soldier stationed in Deggendorf, Bavaria. I met Hans in the camp we are now administrating. You may write to him at my address.

    Sincerely,

PFC. Harry M. Schwalb

33696621 A–T Co. 329 Inf.

APO 83, Postmaster NY, NY

━━━━━━━━

Surprisingly, Hans's letter—on the reverse side of the soldier's letter— is written in English.

━━━━━━━━

From Hans Nothmann in Deggendorf Displaced Persons Camp, Germany, to his brother Guenter Nothmann in Lima

22? August 1945

My dears,

    Today I am very glad to have the opportunity of sending you regards. I am living here in a camp of Bayern [Bavaria] and ask you for writing me fondly. I am waiting for the immigration papers to come to you, hoping it will succeed in a short time. Some–times ago I have written a letter to you thinking you got it and a cable last week. I am to forget please to send to me the adress of Gerda [*sic*]. Many regards and kisses especially to mother.

Hans

———

Another way of finding family members after the war was to write to third parties. In this case Hans Nothmann had an address in New York. He wrote to this person, gave vital information about the individual he was trying to reach, and requested that the letter be forwarded. Noteworthy also is the time between when the letter from New York was mailed, October 1945, and when it was received, January 1946, and the fact that food packages were regularly stolen.

———

From Hans Nothmann in Deggendorf, Germany, to Gerda (Nothmann) Colbert in New York

Mrs. Gerda Colbert *née* Nothmann
Born November 25, 1909 in Gleiwitz, Upper Silesia
Emigrated December 1938 from Berlin, currently in New York
Dear Gerda,

Unfortunately I haven't been able so far to get your address. A good acquaintance, Mrs. Seligmann, has graciously offered to help find your address through her children who live in New York.

I am living here in a camp in Deggendorf (Lower Bavaria) and am waiting for a possibility to emigrate. Unfortunately without Vera and the child, who have perished in the gas chambers of Auschwitz. Also my parents-in-law and Elly have not survived Auschwitz. I was taken from Auschwitz to the Sachsenhausen concentration camp (Oranienburg) and stayed there until the end. I was already in Theresienstadt on December 1st, 1941. This means I have spent almost 4 years in concentration camps. In spite of inquiries I made, I have not been able to find out anything about Herbert.

I received a telegram from Guenter last July but haven't heard from him since even though I have written many letters. Most probably my mail is not reaching him. In any case I was so happy that they and our dear mother are fine. Hope the same is the case with you and only hope that these lines will reach you, then I can write you in more detail. Many regards to your husband.

Kisses from your brother Hans

From Hans Nothmann to Gerda (Nothmann) Colbert

25 January 1946
Camp Deggendorf / Bavaria

Dear Gerda, dear Werner!

I have finally gotten the long-awaited news from you, your letter of 13 October 45 and the enclosed letter from Lima dated 6 October 45. The only sign of life I had had was a telegram from Guenter in August of last year. Since then I have sent several letters and telegrams, not only from here, but also from Czechoslovakia, where I went again in the hope of finding out something about what had happened to Vera and Renate [who were also sent to Theresienstadt]. What I figured out from different sources has led me to the definite conclusion that Vera and Renate were killed on July 11, 1944, in the gas chambers of Auschwitz. The steps I have taken to find Herbert's whereabouts have so far been without success; I have no hope any more.

I have not been in Berlin and do not intend to go. Quite apart from practical considerations, which I would not recommend, I do not want to go back to that city where my every step would remind me of a past that cannot be repaired.

Now let me tell you about my plans: Above all I want out of Germany, the sooner the better. Initially my intention was to go wherever I would be given the opportunity, either New York or Lima. If you have survived 4 years of concentration camps, as I have, nothing else can happen to you in this world. But now that I have heard from you that our dear mother is moving to you, I wish to come to NY! I'm counting on your help! But I also hope that one day I will be in a situation to thank you by paying you back for your willingness to help me. I intend to wait here in Deggendorf until my immigration papers are ready. I am in charge of the car park [garage-chief] of the local UNRRA [United Nations Relief and Rehabilitation Administration, set up for the relief of war victims] and have to work from morning till late at night. I do not lack food; however, I have very little civilian clothing and would be grateful to you for any item. I did not get the food parcel you mentioned you were sending. The new American consulate in Munich was supposed to open on 16.1.46. Unfortunately, it has remained just a promise. As soon as a consulate is working here, I'll let you know. However I would ask you to take the necessary steps immediately with full force.

I was very happy to hear from you, that you are relatively well, and ask you to please add pictures of yourselves in your next letter. I am enclosing one of myself. I would also like to have a picture of our dear mother. By chance I also got pictures of Vera and Renate in Prague. I hope to hear back from you soon and please send the mail for me to the return address on this letter.

Always, your Hans

P.S. Dear Gerda, let me know what our friends are doing, and if you get a chance, greet them all for me. Hans Rosenthal, Schura Silberger, Max Langner, Schimmels. I would be happy to get mail from them.

Kisses, Hans

═══════════

Hans appears to be resilient, but is he really? In his letters, he deals in a matter-of-fact way with Vera and Renate's deaths, as well as with the knowledge that his eldest brother is certainly also dead. This is what has happened. Period. Yet he clearly notes that it would be too painful for him to return to Berlin where he would be reminded of them constantly. Interestingly he notes that the past cannot be "repaired," a verb that is not used in this way except in the Hebrew expression "tikkun olam" (to repair the world), the commandment to behave and act positively.

Hans then makes plans for his future. He wants to leave Germany as soon as possible; he will await his immigration papers in the DP camp because there he has work; he will repay his sister and brother-in-law whenever he can. Only when he writes about the photographs he has found of his wife and daughter and the photographs he requests of his sister, brother-in-law, and mother, do we see a chink in the armor. Hans also sends a picture of himself. It is a reaffirmation of life: "Here I am."

Walter was important in every aspect of our family. Whenever there was a problem, Walter found a solution. In the case of

Regina's children, her son Guenter was a manager in the Lima company; daughter-in-law Thea landed in southern Peru, Walter got her to Lima and later offered her a job she did not accept. But it was his behavior toward his cousin Hans/John that was without parallel. Just as he had planned, Hans Nothmann and Dita, his second wife, moved to New York. With Walter as his silent partner, Hans and his sister Gerda opened H. John Northman, Shirtmakers, at 11 East 57th Street, steps from Fifth Avenue. Walter put up all the capital, and his generosity allowed John to pick up the pieces and start again. Frank Nothmann writes, "John and Dita had Walter and Erna's wedding picture framed and displayed in their Great Neck, NY, house."

Hans Nothmann, now called John Northman, and his wife Dita. New York, 1950s.

The window of H. John Northman, Shirtmakers, 11 East 57th Street, New York City.

I remember visiting the store, but others have much more vivid memories. The elegant shirt store made such an impression on the adolescent mind of John's nephew Jack Nothmann that fifty years later he still remembers the phone number starting with Murray Hill. When she was fourteen years old, Walter's daughter Helen met John and Dita shortly after they arrived in New York. To this day she has a distinct recollection of the numbers the Nazis had tattooed on their forearms. Every concentration camp inmate had such a tattooed number and John's number also appears on the Deggendorf ID card under the rubric "Bearing number."

Hans had learned how to sew inside Auschwitz, where he made uniforms for the Nazis. Gerda was a professional clothing designer who had her own line of children's clothing in New York. Between them, the store prospered. It was such a success that with Walter's financial backing, they opened a second store in the Plaza Hotel managed by Gerda's husband. For reasons we don't know, the second store was soon closed.

All of Walter's shirts were made by cousin Hans / John.

But not all of our letters document such positive outcomes. In addition to Regina's letters and her son Hans's correspondence, we have a letter with its corresponding envelope that was returned to Lima as well as a cable that was never delivered. Both were sent from Lima by Regina's daughter-in-law, Thea, to her father in Berlin. He had been forced to move out of his own apartment into a shared apartment in an area meant for Jews, and his mail was never forwarded. Because the mail was not forwarded, he perished. The element of luck cannot be exaggerated. Whereas Regina, who left in 1941 when it was almost impossible to find a boat, made it to safety, Jacob Gehr did not get to use his Peruvian visa and survive. From German sources, we know that he was transported to Theresienstadt but nothing beyond that. We do not have a place or a time for his death.

In times of crisis, what is important becomes very clear. In her letter Thea requests photographs, especially those of her late mother, and indicates the ongoing work to bring her brother-in-law and family to Lima. The only other items on her wish list, medicine and bedding, were not available in Lima.

───────────────

From Guenter and Thea (Gehr) Nothmann in Lima to Thea's father Jakob Gehr in Berlin

13 November 1941—Nothmann,
Lima-Peru. PO Box 597

My beloved good Papa,

We just received your letter dated 23 October and were hoping that it would include confirmation that you received our telegram. We had actually sent it on that same day, informing you about your

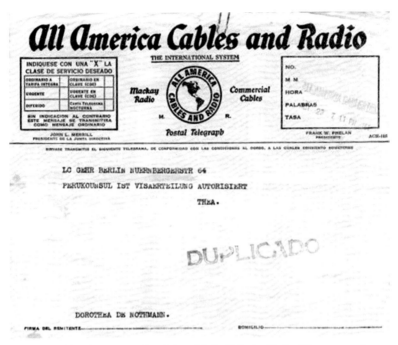

The cable Thea sent to her father, Jakob Gehr, in Berlin. The text reads,
"Peruvian Consul has been authorized to issue visa. Thea."

immigration visa. They may have crossed each other but in any
case we're so happy to have news from you. Hopefully you have
already taken the necessary steps and have the Peru visa in your
passport.

Please be as efficient as Regina and make all the arrangements
as quickly as possible. We just received a telegram that confirms the
arrival of some passengers to Cuba, including Regina, so things
seem to be moving fast. Now it will take only 2–3 weeks for her to
get here and then they will have made it.

Fortunately some people here have been able to get immigration papers for their parents; it's still blocked for other family
members. But we have to be happy to have been able to accomplish

this much and our thoughts are still with all those whom we wish to help.

We also got a telegram from my brother-in-law Hans and family asking us to arrange his immigration as soon as possible. I have already done all I can and things are progressing. It still remains to be seen whether I will be able to do this and how long it will take but one does whatever is humanly possible.

Ferdi also has the visa for Betty and you may be talking to her as she needs to travel to Berlin in order to get the visa. With some good luck, the two of you may be able to travel together, which would be a great relief for us. Meanwhile you may have heard that Mr. Becker has also gotten a visa for him and his daughter and maybe you can all travel together. How will we get the news from you that you're departing on a specific date? We can hardly wait for that day.

You write that you have only one suit; that of course is bad. Should your wardrobe be too much of an issue just go as you are and we'll get you things here. It would certainly be an advantage if you have a summer suit since the hot season here is starting now and lasts until April. For the trip you will definitely need a travel cover or some kind of blanket.

Daddy, if you can take your down bedding with you please don't forget it; we have only one pillow and one blanket each since we can't afford down bedding, it's very costly here. Should you have some spare bed linen and towels, bring them with you but don't bring anything that is torn as things here fall apart quickly and it only makes sense to bring things in good condition. Medicines are also very expensive, so bring whatever you can. Shoes are not expensive here and our friend Namm manages the largest shoe factory so you will never have to go barefoot. Guenter has plenty of socks and can give you some. Please bring all family pictures with you, especially any pictures you can find of our beloved mom, may she rest in peace. I don't have even one souvenir of our beloved mother, not even one bad picture. Other than this I'm sure I don't need to remind you not to bring any unnecessary junk. It will just cost you transportation money and in any case you were never inclined to keep old things.

Now I'd like to ask you to help Marta in any way possible. We owe her a lot of gratitude as she has had more trouble than joy with our family lately. You may rest assured that I will do anything possible to help her. The way things are at the moment this is difficult, but with time we will get good advice.

As you can see, who would have thought that you would get your visa as fast as you did, and surprisingly enough it went faster than we thought. It will be difficult for you to say farewell to the many loved ones who have cared for you lately. However, I'm convinced that they have all wished this for you and I can assure you that we will do our utmost to offer you a good life here.

Hopefully everything will continue its good course here and we shall be able to help many more people. Yesterday we got a letter from Falcks. Anni writes that they're fine and that she will send a photo soon.

I'll close for now as I still want to write Marta a few lines. Take care of all the steps with the greatest calm but as fast as possible.

Be healthy and write to us immediately as we want to know how things are going regarding your departure. Regards to all the loved ones around you. Receive the most intimate hugs and kisses

from your children, Thea and Guenter

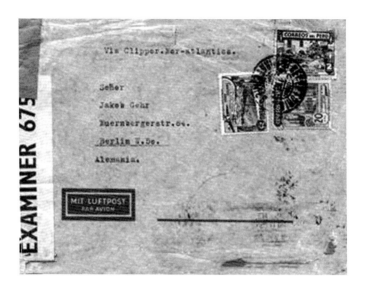

The envelope containing the letter Thea wrote to her father that was returned to sender.

CHAPTER EIGHT

A Cup of Bean Coffee
Is Medicine for Me

Postwar Requests, 1946–1950

FROM the postwar years there are requests for money and thank-you letters for care packages. Fritz Lustig writes from Shanghai, where some 18,000 Jews lived, having fled Nazism in the late 1930s and early 1940s. The other letters are from West Germany, East Germany, and Poland. One is from a family friend; several are from Erna's long-time friend Angela and her brother. The terrible post-war period, where hunger and dislocation pervaded Europe, is evident. The letters are in German with one exception. Angela writes three letters in English but inserts words and sometimes entire sentences in German. One of her letters even has several sentences in Italian. I have made no corrections to her letters. Presumably she thought the Polish censors didn't know much English, or perhaps she was simply trying to perfect her skills.

From Fritz Lustig in Shanghai to his cousin Erna (Lustig) Neisser and Walter Neisser in Lima

18 December 1945

Friedrich Lustig, Shanghai, C/o Hicom POB 1425

Dear Erna, dear Mr. Neisser,

On September 16th I wrote you a letter, but because I don't know if you received it (I sent it with an American pilot), I am writing a second time.

Since we have not heard from each other, I am curious to know how all of you are. I hope that these lines will find you in good health. To tell you how we have been in these times would be very long. But I do want to tell you a few things. After finding comfortable lodgings, we had to abandon them because the Japanese locked us up in a ghetto. During that long period it was impossible to make a living and we had only what the JOINT gave us. But living from that was impossible and we often had to sell our possessions to satisfy our hunger. In the many years we have been here, we have been unable to find work and now have very few belongings left. We are tormented not only by the Japanese, but one good day our friends, the Americans, bombed us, leaving many of ours dead. To describe all of this would be horrific and you must have read about it in your newspapers.

We now live in "peace" and are tormented by the Chinese. Two days ago they published a decree saying that Germans, Austrians, and Jews must be repatriated with the shortest delay possible. Not only is the voyage a problem but they are also discriminating against us and using the same decree for us and the Germans. All the immigrants are rising up and all fear for their future, for we do not know what will happen to us. They want to annihilate us commercially.

Dear Mr. Neisser, can you give me advice, what [kind of business] can I start? Do you think it is reasonable that we return to Germany? Staying here is impossible. Would it be advisable to emigrate again and start again at zero? You would do me a great favor by advising me as soon as possible since the UNNRA is beginning to register people at this moment. We have a grave problem and don't know what the outcome will be.

My wife is not well here. The fault lies with the climate. She has already been operated twice here and the doctors blame the local weather. Our son Heinz does everything possible to ease our situation but his income is not sufficient to feed three people. He is hard working and disciplined but there is no future for him here. "Asia for the Asians."

I have no news of my sister Else [Sack] and her husband. I do not know where they both are nor if they are still alive. Despite all my questions to my sister Paula and to Walter Sack in Sweden, I have not been able to find out where the two are. I would like to ask, my dear Erna, how is your dear mother and your dear children? Have you had any news about some of our relatives? If so, I beg you to transmit it to me since I am greatly interested.

For you, dear Mr. Neisser, I have another petition. Now that I have described what has happened to us and how we now are faring, I beg you to provide help in some way. Would it be possible that you might ease our heavy lives until we are again on our feet in Germany or some other place? For seven years we have suffered what destiny has given us but we still have the will to start again and therefore have a more bearable life. If you could support me with some money, be assured that I will consider it a loan and will return it at the first opportunity. Do not be annoyed with this request, dear Mr. Neisser, but you can understand my present situation.

I close these lines and wish you, dear Mr. Neisser, all the best. For you, dear Erna, your dear mother and your dear children, I wish the same and say good-bye with affectionate greetings.

Your cousin Fritz

Dear Mally and dear Heinz also send affectionate greetings.

Sender: Friedrich Lustig

C/ HICOM

Postbox 1425

Shanghai, China

This letter has a note in red pencil, in Walter's handwriting, that says "$50.00" [US], which today would be worth around $650. In this case Walter did not show the generosity he so lavishly bestowed on others, despite this and previous requests from Fritz himself and various other relatives on his behalf. Perhaps Walter never forgave him for lying or perhaps Fritz really was a rascal he did not want to help. Fritz Lustig's story is incomplete. We know he went to the United States but since then he has fallen out of sight and nothing has been heard from him.

From Hermann Jacoby in Berlin to Erna (Lustig) Neisser in Lima

21 June 1947

Berlin NW, 21,

[East Germany] den 21/6/47 Bochumerstr. 27, v IV

My dear Mrs. Neisser!

We have not heard from each other for a long time and many horrors have occurred in the meantime. But look! I survived it and am now 76 years old.

Life is hard, very hard. My wife has been at my daughter's in Hamburg for over two years and cannot return until the borders are opened. She went to Hamburg shortly before the division of Berlin, and there was surprised by the events and could no longer come back. I have suffered a great deal; the house was bombed shortly before the end [of the war]. I survived miraculously and came away alive and now sit in the remains of the house. Half the house was torn away.

But now I can sleep in peace. No bombs are falling and what was much worse, no more fear of the Gestapo. But I don't want to complain a lot to you. That is over. What is not over yet is the hunger. I hope that you and your dear ones have been well in all these years we have not heard from each other and that you are in good health. How are your children? They must be grown up by now, and your husband and your dear mother? All of that interests me. Give me the pleasure in this joyless time and send me as quickly as possible, by airmail, a complete report. And if you could add a small picture, I would be especially pleased.

Should it be possible for you to send me something edible, I would obviously be especially grateful to you. I imagine you have many responsibilities, but believe me, the need here is great and every small thing helps. The doctor has told me my body mostly needs fats and other nourishing foods, like for example chocolate, cocoa, etc. Also a cup of bean coffee is medicine for me. I don't want you to spend a lot on my behalf and am grateful for the smallest things, I can use everything.

Please do not be angry at my request for foodstuffs from an old friend and a childhood friend of your late father. I remember you often and I hope that you, too, sometimes recall me after all of this time we have not heard from each other. In old friendship, I remain with many hearty greetings,

your Hermann Jacoby

———————

Again our information is incomplete. We don't know if Walter and Erna sent him a care package or what subsequently befell Mr. Jacoby.

The letter that follows, written over a two-month period by Gerhard Schymiczek, has sections that read more like a magazine article than a personal letter. Gerhard is the brother of Angela, Erna's long-time friend, whom he calls Gela. She is back in Gleiwitz, now Gliwice, Poland, while he is in Bavaria. He analyzes the European situation like a political scientist, giving examples, stating facts, relating pertinent details. The picture he paints is devastating, especially his comments on the German economy and the Russian occupation. In addition, he has a great deal of information about the Jewish community in Gleiwitz, one he and his sister obviously knew intimately. He speaks of his job as a bank employee, but it is clear that he is a highly educated man, one the bank used to draft briefing papers for the Foreign Minister. Although Angela writes several letters in 1950, three years after this one, there is no mention of her brother and his family. What became of the tubercular Gerhard and his family is another unknown.

———————

From Gerhard Schymiczek (Angela's brother) to Erna (Lustig) Neisser, Walter Neisser, and Fanny Lustig

2 March 1947

Regensburg [West Germany]

Dear Mrs. Erna! Dear Mr. Neisser! Dear Mrs. Lustig!

Yesterday, to our great joy and surprise, we received your parcel, sent by you via the International Gift Parcel Service, totally intact. It included: 1 cured sausage, sweet dry milk, 1 lb. coffee, ¼ lb. tea, ½ lb. chocolate, 1 can sardines in oil, 1 can scraped bacon, 1 lb. honey, 1 lb. butter, 1 lb. cheese, 2 bags noodles, 40 Camel cigarettes, and a rubber hot water bottle. You cannot imagine what joy we felt. Just one week ago, we were informed about the new cutbacks in rations. Accordingly, <u>for a 4-week period</u>, one grown-up receives, instead of 1000 grams, only 600 grams of meat and only 200 grams of butter or margarine, instead of 250. The bread ration is set at 6 kilos and the increase we received during the winter, 4.75 kilos for four weeks, has been postponed until the late shiploads have arrived. In addition, imagine that we must suffer a great deal, for this winter has been especially cold. We can burn only 2 cubic meters of wood in total. We are very lucky to have received 1 metric hundredweight of black coal briquettes [about fifty kilos] . . . The frost boils I started having last year have now appeared on all my fingers to a great degree. For this reason, the parcel represents a big support and will hopefully serve us over the entire critical period. How I have learned to beg: I would never have thought it possible. Yet it has gone well for me, and every day I thank God on my knees that I have found work while many thousands of others doze or vegetate in the country, often under horrendous conditions.

Perhaps, as was suggested shortly before Christmas, the bank might transfer me elsewhere and I will have to move away from here. Surely our suffering is far from over. We hope that the many

Germans who are with the occupation army may return to their former homes and situations, and [we] will be able to judge [the situation] better. [We don't want a situation] like in 1920 when the French army arrived in Upper Silesia with their Alps corps because they thought that otherwise they would not be able to climb our mountains. That gives us, the people from Gleiwitz, the courage to withstand even the most inhuman conditions that we endure in this otherwise blessed land, Bavaria. This year again, our house is totally wet, up to [and including] the baseboards, even though Mizzi [my wife] cooks by an open window despite the terrible cold, so that the fumes go outside . . . Then the question arises, what will we find when the march home begins? Doors and windows are gone, at least door and window handles, all heating removed, not to speak of the bathroom and toilet installations. What will the Poles, with their well-known love for Germans, leave for us? We will have to start all over again. Gela and mother do not have the house in their possession. They are paying rent to live in their own home. My sister-in-law Dore [the wife of Erwin, Angela and Gerhard's brother] and her daughter Verena still deliver bread rolls early in the morning. Verena goes to school, Gela teaches like she did before.

Verena shows great intelligence and has an outstanding voice; she already helps by teaching piano and giving beginners voice lessons even though she is only 16 years old. Gela writes with great pride that it will be child's play for Verena . . . . It is depressing for her that [our brother] Erwin has not sent or has not been able to send any news from his jail in Russia. Who knows if he is still alive?

Oh, untold numbers of our acquaintances are dead and we could spend the whole day crying, thinking of those many dear people. I have recently heard that at the very end Director Anspach was gassed in Auschwitz and, I believe, along with him Justizrat

[Judge] Kochmann and Rabbi Dr. Ochs. They were the last ones from Gleiwitz, who at the end of 1943 were taken to Theresienstadt in Bohemia. In late 1944, they were transported from there to Auschwitz. Sadly they could not be saved. On the other hand, lawyer Schlesinger is still in Gleiwitz as well as San.-Rat. [honorary doctor's title] Blumenfeld. Both are working tirelessly helping those who are returning in these crazy times. Blumenfeld lived at the corner of Wilhempplatz and Wilhemstrasse. The damage to the city is terrible. To get back at the stupid HJ [Hitler] Youth, they shot a high-ranking Russian officer in front of Upper Silesia House when the Russian occupation began. The [event] provoked terrible reprisals against the population. Among the Nazis and others, thousands committed suicide because they could no longer flee. [Such was the case of] a big Nazi, the Upper Studies director Grosser and his wife and friend (cyanide). Yet many Nazis escaped in time and now are sitting in the English and American zones, their money safely put away, as cheeky as the local Nazis. It is a great sadness that this rabble have made themselves comfortable and continue damaging our good name.

The occupation forces often say that we do not deserve their help. But on the other hand, how can a democratic government do a good job, when, in view of the above, they cut us back everywhere, when all the countries clamor for German coal and German wood so nothing is left for us. We will be totally ruined for many decades and it will simply no longer be viable to live here. How will we find the courage to put this pigsty in good order? For me, a practicing Christian, it is unthinkable that the victors want to force us on a road to total ruination. For that reason, I hope and pray every day that the victors don't fall victim to radical Bolshevism, which would be the same as imposing an Asian lifestyle run wild.

The Balkans would be golden compared to this. Right now it looks terribly bad; boundless selfishness is celebrating its cruel triumph.

Of course those who suffer the most are the children, but one can do so little to help. Every day after work, I spend at least two or three hours trying to counter this misery. So I am usually dead tired when, around midnight, I seek my bed, only to rise again by 6. Only God knows how long I will be able to keep this up with my poor health, well known to you. In any case, I would consider myself a villain if I did nothing but fight my tuberculosis, without thinking of the suffering of others. Until now God has given me the strength. I hope it will continue. Even Gela has collapsed, but is all right again. I will write her how kind you have been to think of us. In any case, I still hope to hear from you. [Tell me] how you are and whether and when you have received my message. Apparently nobody in the Kornblum family survived. Grete, like Lilli and Dante, is long dead, and Lotte has disappeared without a trace.

I am so pleased to have gotten hold of a new [typewriter] ribbon. 30.3.1947

This letter, which I wanted to send you right away, sat for four weeks. In the meantime, I had a terrible cold with terrible bronchitis, and in addition, sinusitis. I had to doctor myself for four weeks. Finally I have gotten over it. As you can imagine the hot water bottle and the honey did invaluable service. First we had a little dry wood for heating, but later only very wet wood and the old museum piece we have for a stove has its quirks. Happily that is now over and the outside temperature is above 0 C. so that even if it is sometimes chilly, we are not freezing.

Meanwhile, one of the bank employees who was a prisoner of war has been released and has returned to the bank. So now the next worry begins, who will have to go? I or the second refugee the bank employs? Then, when the no-longer-brown Nazis come back, it will be over in any case since they are still given preferential treatment. There is no law to prepare for the return of the old Nazis that would protect us refugees from losing our means of livelihood. The existing provisions have too many loopholes and allow them employment in what is called "ordinary work." The only one who does <u>not</u> do "ordinary work" at a bank is the branch director. Everybody else does "ordinary work." If the military government could have seen the filth that made up the heads of the banks when they enforced this principle, they would have immediately withdrawn their consent. Unfortunately one cannot foresee everything.

We participated in the preparatory work for the Foreign Ministers Conference, and the materials were to be transmitted to the gentlemen in order to ensure that the eastern frontiers question be guaranteed. We hope that the statistics we have provided will restore Silesia to its pre-1938 border. It is quite obvious that the Poles will never be able to farm this rich land the way it should be [farmed]. Imagine, the entire 1945 crop was left to rot on the stalks because no one was there to harvest it. Also in Czechoslovakia, much remained on the stalks. . . .

Of course, all of this is the same [kind of] public mischief as in the Hitler years. But you know the situation in Czechoslovakia, in Poland, and in Upper Silesia well. I don't have to elaborate. You will already have thought these things anyway. We now hope that the view of the U.S. and British military governments about the real situation has become so clear that they will not be deceived by the dissimulating Poles and the Czechs, who want to be powerful players. It is not who owns the land, but who is capable of cultivating it. Many volumes will be written about the war and postwar development when, beside the madness of the Hitler years, much must be said about the unpleasantness in the Poles' and Czechs' methods. We hope and pray that our homes [in Upper Silesia] will be returned under British or American control. Under Russian sovereignty, we can expect nothing. In her last letter Gela writes that for example the Russians pay 8.00 Zloty for a ton of coal, and in Gliwice, for the same ton, she has to pay 750.00. No comment necessary. <u>Then</u> of course the reparations received by Russia amount to nothing. We want to work here and hope.

Now I want to close. Best wishes, many warm greetings, many thanks, and a request. [Please tell us] if your dear mother is still alive and how she is.

Sincerely, Gerhard Schymiczek and wife Mizzi, [my daughter] Hedi Maiss and [my son] Edwin, who will now attend a hotel school in Munich. He starts after Easter. Edwin knows English almost perfectly but must now learn French, Italian, and Spanish very quickly. For French and Italian I obtained both dictionaries and exercise books, of course not in a bookstore but privately owned and on loan. But for Spanish we have no prospects for finding anything. How we have come down. The land of the book has no textbooks, no exercise books, no stationery, nor envelopes. For someone who has been away from Germany for 10 years, it is unimaginable. Mizzi wants to make a cooking box, to save on gas and firewood in the summer time. There are no nails and no boxes. So again one has to "organize" for weeks. Best greetings again.

━━━━━━━

By 1950, Angela is back in Gleiwitz, now part of Poland and called Gliwice. Her four letters, written in an eight-month period in 1950, paint an even bleaker picture. They give news of what has befallen family and friends as well as information about the last Jews of Gleiwitz. It is clear that Angela understood the importance of Rudy and Maruca Lustig in the lives of Walter and Erna, for she mentions their death in Buenos Aires in 1949. But much more importantly, her brother Erwin has most probably died, and Angela supports her mother, sister-in-law, and two nieces with her meager earnings as a piano teacher, singer, and accompanist.

From Angela Schymiczek in Gliwice (Gleiwitz) to Erna (Lustig) Neisser in Lima [Letter written in English]

12 March 1950
Gliwice

My dear Erna!

2 weeks ago I got your dear letter in date of 11.II.—I thank you heartiest for all your good news. You will be persuaded that all your letters are beams of light from another world, wherein I only can fly in dreams. I am laughing to hear that you are so much travelling. Today in Italy—tomorrow in Lima and now in New York and so on. What a pity that I haven't a husband like Walter. I like travelling for my life and don't feel me old—but young—healthy and now I must sit down. . . .

Erna Erna, please, send me a foto of your family. I wish to have you all here by me. To make a foto is not so expensive for you like for us here. Your last letter has been opened in Posen $ haven't been in. But I hope that it has been o.k., because you wrote that you mailed for me some Nylons. I hope also they will arrive!!

The last 3 weeks I had many difficulties with my dwelling because each person must have only sixteen [square] meters and mother and myself we have 104. But now I put all right, because I need 2 rooms for my profession. Now I have been in Katowice just 3X for my new legitimation card of art and culture!! Wednesday I must go there once again.

The life isn't easy, but I must remain strong. When I become weak—all my family would be lost.—Verena is working in the chemical laboratorium. . . . The work isn't good for her. Mother is ever weak, but I am contented—she is still with me!—I only am living for my family and I must work from early to late—in order to gain the daily bread.

That Maruca and Rudy [Lustig] died is a great lost for your whole family. They were a kind remembering of happy hours.— This last night died Mrs. Dr. Blumenfeld. [On] the 1. III. she had an apoplexy, then a little vein burst in the brain.+ Now the Dr. with 80 years, remains alone.

Now my dear Erna, I remain with heartiest wishes for yours and your whole family's healthy and with many greetings + kisses in love

yours, mother, Dore, Verena, Roswitha

From Angela Schymiczek in Gliwice (Gleiwitz) to Erna (Lustig) Neisser in Lima [Letter written in English. The words and phrases in the original German are in italics.]

29 May 1950

My dear Erna,

I hope you got all my letters.—Exactly before the Whitsuntide your parcel from New York arrived. What a fun and delight to open it. Like a *"box of surprises"* from the reach [sic] uncle of America. We are all like children also being hundred years old. The parcel were opened at Gdynia, Pol. [Gedingen] then put in a sack, sealed. When the postman brought it, I must open it alone and give back the sack. Then I saw contents. There have been in: 1 dress, 1 pair of shoes, 3 pair of stockings, 1 pair of old over-shoes, 2 pantaloons (white), 1 corset, a pair of green woolen gloves, one pair of Teddy-fur shoes, and an aeroplan—the delight of Roswitha—for us to make a flight to America.

Dear Erna, I thank you heartiest for all this wonderful things— also in the name of all my dears. God bless you, Walter, your children and the whole family! The dress is a little to wide, but that doesn't matter. I am so happy at it. I look very nice in it . . . . Here one cann't get patent leather-shoes and they are so elegant! They will be my elegantest shoes and when Verena need them, I'll lend them to her. Dear Erna, you may laugh—but all this last 5½ years I couldn't buy nothing, neither dresses nor shoes. What we safed under the ashes and earth in the garden, we keep like gold!! Always new and elegant—old things made new!! This is a great art. I make my dresses alone, with the help and advice of my dear mother. So your old coat (parcel of 1947) became a wonderful model, like of a very good dressmaker! But I needed 2½ months because I could every day only two hours work at it. Your grey shoes are still very fashionable and going on the street, they are always looked at. The Nylons are a "miraculum" for us. We cann't buy them . . . . The slippers will be my best comrades when in the 'winter coldness' I must sit at the piano . . .

Dr. Blumenfeld has now a *housekeeper*, one of my acquaintances, widow of a director of Deichsel, now poor. Dr. Schlesinger must leave our town to the Russian Zone. But perhaps they get a per-mission to American Zone, Frankfurt a/Main—where the sons of his wife have just a dwelling. Dear Erna, in the next days I'll visit Father Sally [Erna's father Salomon] and all friends on the ciment-ery—church yard.

For to-day all our heartiest and pious wishes. We pray every day for you all. To mother Lustig, Neisser, all your dears, our kind-est regards. Specially to uncle Max. I embrace you and remain with kisses and greetings and thank givings and love

your Angela, mother, Dore, Verena, Roswitha

[Side of page 2] *With the stockings you did well, (I) didn't have to pay any duty only for shoes 500.00, a total of 775.00, so very little !!!*

From Angela Schymiczek in Gliwice (Gleiwitz) to Erna (Lustig) Neisser in Lima [Letter mostly in German with some English.]

25 June 1950

My dear Erna,

I'll hope you received all my letters and also the last, wherein I confirmed the receipt of your parcel from New York. I am so glad at it. Two weeks ago I have been in a symphonical concert and I dressed your blue dress. I look very nice in it. I gathered the sleeves a little . . .

On the 12.6 Dr. Schlesinger and his wife left on an emigrant transport for Germany. At present they are in a camp in the Rus-sian Zone and hope to be let through to go to a Jewish old people's home in Frankfurt am Main, in the American Zone. Dr. Blumen-feld wept like a child when they said good-bye. They were the only surviving Jews of Gleiwitz and had strong ties to each other. I hope that Ernst Auszach,[?] as Chief of Military Police, will be able to help his mother's cousin Dr. Schlesinger. I just don't know if he was recalled from Munich and Wiesbaden and is again in

New York. In New York, Cantor Cohn is again active as a cantor. The colleague from my studies, Stefan Frenkel, the violin virtuoso, is with the Metropolitan Orchestra in New York, son-in-law of Mühlen–Danziger.

On the 13.7 Brauers leave for Palestine. He is the nephew of a big priest? They fled from Rybnik to Siberia; came back in 45; they live in the apartment above yours, together with Mrs. Schles[inger]. Rutka Brauer started [studying piano] with Verena and now practices very diligently with me. She is 11 years old, plays Mozart sonatas, Chopin preludes very nicely. They have relatives in America, Australia, and Palestine who are wealthy and influential who will continue to help them. We have close ties with them and the leave-taking will be painful. One after the other leaves the old homeland and one gets more and more lonely. We still claw at this old earth, like a farmer to his native soil. Will we too have to reach for the walking stick? Quo vadis? Where are you going? Fate.

Horizontal: Regards to all your dear ones. I embrace you and give you my heartfelt wishes and greetings with a kiss in love,

Yours Angela

[P.S.] Dr. Schlesinger has reached the English Zone.

From Angela Schymiczek in Gliwice (Gleiwitz) to Erna (Lustig) Neisser in Lima [Letter written in English. The words and phrases in the German original, as well as words and phrases in Italian, are in italics.]

12 October 1950

My dear Erna!

For your kind letter in date of 21.III I thank you heartiest. It has been intact, also the 2 $ pictures! God may recompense you and your family! In the first letter of February 11 you wrote to me of "some Nylons" you mailed to me, but until to-day I didn't get nothing. But perhaps you didn't send them off. Please write to me about this fact, because I must inquire—if you sent them realy.

You cann't imagine how glad I am hearing that you with [?] were at the Metropolitan and heard Heifetz. I remember all my good times—*tempi passati*—times past—but so I know that still to-day abroad one lives the old life! But I only can fly there in my dreams. Please let me take part on your travelling, on your life—writing to me. I work . . . Musik, religion and good books—this let us support the hard life. Didn't you see the first Violinist of Metropolitan, Stefan Frenkel. He was studying with me at the Academy of Berlin (1920-23) and his wife was the daughter of Mühlen-Danziger, Gleiwitz. Please to give them all my kindest regards.

I wished to know your children, my dear Erna. I knew them only like babies. Tito seemed to become father "Sally" [like his grandfather Salomon]. Now they are upgrown men—*cavaliere.* Because I have no own children, I only think of Verena and Roswitha. Verena is very intelligent. You must hear playing of Chopin Etudes. With tears in my eyes I am listening her and I only regret Erwin can't hear and see his daughter. The poor good boy!! . . . I am in great fear about the health of the 2 children because we haven't here the good medicines. Please Erna, help me to safe the life of 2 real very intelligent and good children!

For to-day I'll finish, it is 24 o'clock—midnight. I thank you hearties also in the name of my whole family and remain with [the rest is in Italian]*, many cordial greetings and kisses and angels linings for the welfare of you and your whole family always your faithful friend, with much love.*

Your Angela, *Mother,* Dore, Verena *and* Roswitha

The contrast between the lives described in these letters and life in Lima could not be greater. The family in Lima flourished, their prosperity evident. The pictures show that both at work and in the community, all was well. The first photographs are work related, others are of social gatherings, and the last one is a Jewish community function.

Walter left, Guenter Nothmann right.

One of the Neisser and Co. stores at night.

A Neisser Regalos staff party.

Walter is seated in the center. Standing to his left Heinz Liebermann, behind him Curt Nothmann (called tio Huevo, Uncle Egg, because of the shape and baldness of his head). Standing from left Franz Herzka, Willy Simenauer, and Guenter Nothmann. Standing behind and to the right of Walter, Erich Neisser and Friedrich Freund.

As usual, Walter is in the center of the picture, surrounded by La 1870 community leaders. Michael Siegel served as spiritual leader of La 1870 from 1941 to 1957, when the first rabbi was hired. A lawyer by training, the brilliant and cultured Dr. Siegel arrived in Lima in 1940. He found work in a bookstore, then had part-time employment with the community. Although he was not a rabbi, he led services, taught the children, and prepared boys and girls for bar and bat mitzvahs. In the early years, the congregation held the services in German and Hebrew, and slowly added in Spanish. The congregation considered itself Conservative but had many aspects of Reform Judaism. Only in the 1950s was Dr. Siegel able to resume his work as a German lawyer. He represented members of the community and helped file claims for the *Wiedergutmachung*, the reparations Germany paid to the victims of Nazi persecution. Because the claimants no longer had the documents or deeds required to prove their losses, the forms were long and complicated. I remember my mother spending many hours filling them out with the patient Dr. Siegel.

In the postwar years, La 1870 community numbered some 500 people. There were conferences, concerts, weddings, and more, all well attended. The seats on the board were always contested, with several groups running slates; and the women's committee was very active. Because they needed a place in Miraflores for both religious services and community events, La 1870 worked out a unique arrangement with the Anglo-American Society (Sociedad Anglo Americana / Beneficiencia Británica). For Saturday religious services, La 1870 used a rental space known as the Social Hall, while the Anglo-American Society used it for their services on Sundays. This rental arrangement worked well as long as the High Holidays did not fall on a Sunday, when the Social Hall was unavailable, but

Walter with his sales manager, his niece Ruth Angress.

Walter is third from the left with Erna beside him.

A Jewish community gathering with Walter, wearing a bow tie, in the center. Erna is standing directly behind him. Beside her, Michael Siegel. Kurt and Margot Berger are seated at the far left.

all too often the community was forced to rent a movie theater a few blocks away. By 1948 the community was affluent enough to buy the building and the furnishings, and today, entirely rebuilt, it still serves as both synagogue and community offices.

We used the Anglo-American Society furnishings. The main room had long benches entirely covered by two red cushions, one to sit on, one to lean against. There were crosses on the backs of the benches but no decorations on the walls. For our services the benches were set up in rows, and the women sat on one side, the men on the other. Folding chairs at the end of every bench provided extra seating for the holiday services. Long benches for the children skirted both walls.

The majority of members had now been in Peru about ten years, and they were certainly better established. Many owned their own businesses, houses, and cars, but they lived within the confines of the German-Jewish community. My parents bought bread and pastries at Pastelería Herbert Baruch, a bakery owned by a fellow Yekke. But change was evident, for in addition to the Central European pastries Baruch also baked empanadas, Peruvian meat pies filled with onions, olives, and spices, beloved by his customers' Peruvian-born children. Books in German were available at the Internacional, owned by Mr. Klein. My mother bought and read me the German children's classics: *Max und Moritz*, the terrifying *Struwwelpeter*, and later the adventure novels of Karl May. All my cousins remember their parents doing the same and we do not remember any books in Spanish, children's or adult. Nevertheless the daily newspaper *El Comercio* was, in my father's words, *ausgebetet*, read in its entirety.

To this day all of the members of my generation know a large number of songs in German. We know children's songs, wandering songs, and some of us remember night-time prayers, more chants than songs. All of us, with very few exceptions, cannot carry a tune but know the words to "Das Wandern ist des Müllers Lust" and we can all belt out "Alle meine Entchen" and "Hoppe, Hoppe, Reiter."

I never heard my father or my aunts talk about Beuthen or Gleiwitz in the same way that my mother spoke of her hometown, Karlsbad, Czechoslovakia. She would go on endlessly, recalling the smells of flowers and the taste of fruits not available in tropical Peru, the forest walks she used to take, complete with walking songs. When visitors from her hometown who now lived in Bolivia or Chile came through, they would spend an entire evening reimagining Karlsbad. They would recall a specific street and talk about every shop, what it sold, what the goods looked or tasted like, mentally walking up and down the streets they had been forced to flee. Sometimes, because of the years that had elapsed, their memories would differ and they would argue about whether the butcher was beside the post office or if the coffee house was between them or to the right. During these evenings of nostalgia, my father and I listened without saying a word. He officially dubbed them "Karlsbad evenings."

Thus, integrating into the majority culture was unthinkable. If in their Yekke mentality, my parents already felt superior to the much-maligned Yiddish-speaking Ostjuden, the Jews from the East, then the Peruvians were beyond the pale. They had no Kultur, that Central European culture they held so dear. Although as a child I don't remember ever being specifically told that despite having been born in Peru and holding a Peruvian passport, I was not really a Peruvian, it was always implicit. My close friends were all Jewish, as we said in Spanish, "de la colonia."

Walter, on the other hand, had many friends outside the Jewish community. He would invite them to his country place, sometimes without wives and even without servants. Helen remembers him in the kitchen with his closest friend, the Swiss-Peruvian painter Harry [Heinrich / Enrique] Kleiser, putting oil in a frying pan and adding peas that popped like popcorn and covered the kitchen floor. She recalls that Kleiser and his Peruvian wife had two daughters, the younger of whom, Lilly, was her friend. Once the two men took the girls on a trip to Chimbote, in northern Peru, probably to visit a hydroelectric plant. Walter had other painter friends, some European, others Peruvian. Helen writes:

> The majority of German Jews that I knew in my childhood, family and friends, were a closed group that did not interact with the Peruvians. They spoke German, and although some spoke Spanish very well, most had heavy accents since they had not learned the language in childhood. Their children did not have that problem. My parents, on the other hand, had a large circle of Peruvian friends but never gave up their customs, those profoundly learned like punctuality and honesty. They would not tolerate cheating or lack of honesty and loyalty.

Chapter Nine

The Mediocre in Any Profession Don't Get Very Far

Lima, 1948–1960

THE last twelve years of Walter's life can be neatly divided into summit and decline. During the time that President Manuel Odría was in power, from 1948 to 1954, the business was an astounding success, and Walter continued to have extraordinary energy, running a large multifaceted enterprise, heading the family, dealing with his political contacts, and being a very active philanthropist. He was on the board of the Rotary, had a high rank in the Masons, and in 1954 became the first president of B'nai Brith Peru. Walter and Erna were jet-setters before the term was invented. They traveled to the United States and Europe several times a year, scheduling their trips around a meeting or a trade show, combining business and pleasure. But the few years before Walter's death in 1960 were difficult, with trouble at Neisser and Co. and repeated trips to Boston to see his doctor. Allusions to big changes in his business and family life pepper the letters from that time. But he also deals with personal matters, like my father's heart attack and his intention to wish me a happy seventh birthday in person.

During much of the same period Walter and Erna sent their adolescent children to posh boarding schools in Massachusetts. Helen, aged fourteen, went to Abbot Academy in Andover, Massachusetts, and her two brothers, aged fifteen and sixteen, to the Brooks School in North Andover. Tito had finished high school in Lima and had been accepted at Harvard but Walter felt he was too young and needed to work on his English. Rudy, who had severe dyslexia, had trouble at every school he attended.

Helen writes: "Despite the fact that the two schools were very close, we never saw each other because both schools were very strict. The ties to the family were very weak during that period. Communication with my parents was through a weekly letter, and sometimes even more time elapsed."

All three children were probably sent away at the same time because they hoped Rudy could be better educated in the US. Yet even though they came from elegant schools in Lima, the boarding schools they attended with the children of America's wealthiest citizens must have been a shock. In Lima, where schooling depended on social class and wealth, they had of course attended private schools. Public education was not an option for anyone in the middle or upper classes. Public schools were overcrowded, the teachers ill prepared. All the children in the Jewish community attended private schools.

Although Walter's siblings worked for him and lived close by, they made independent decisions about their children's education. The early preference was for British education. All three of Walter's children first attended Miss Kufal's, later called San Silvestre. Why the boys kept changing schools was most probably related to Rudy's dyslexia, unrecognized at the time. In Peru, a country where 99 percent of the population was Roman Catholic, the good schools were almost all single-gender schools run by various Catholic orders. Starting in grade 4, Helen went to Villa Maria, the most elegant and expensive Catholic nuns' school in the city. The boys went to a Catholic priests' school, Champagnat, and to the Anglo-Peruano, later called San Andrés. The few nondenominational schools were associated with a specific country and taught the language of that country as well as Spanish. The choices ranged from British, Italian, Swiss, French, and American, to German and Japanese, the latter two obviously not options for our family.

When a Jewish school was established in 1946, it became a popular choice, and by the 1950s the vast majority of Jewish children in Lima, 500 at its peak, attended Colegio León Pinelo. That was the case for only one child in our family. Kleine Erna chose the Jewish school for her son, but Kaethe selected a British girls' school, and my parents and Ruth opted for the American school. We did not change schools and were certainly not sent abroad for high school. As a result, we received very different educations, learned different languages, and were instilled with different values and worldviews.

We have well over a hundred letters from this period, the majority to Rudy when he was a high school student in the US Walter and Erna usually wrote separately, although some of her letters have a postscript from him. Walter dictated his letters to his secretary at the office. Whereas all the letters I received when I attended college in the US were entirely in German, Walter and Erna wrote in Spanish with short asides in German and occasional phrases in English. Although Walter tended to micromanage the lives of all of his children and frequently gave them all moral advice, his letters to each one of them are quite distinct.

We have very few letters to Tito, the eldest son, always a model student, studious and obedient. Since his grades were not an issue, Walter wrote to him about business, politics, and family matters.

━━━━━━━━━

From Walter to his son Alberto (Tito) Neisser at Brooks School, North Andover, Massachusetts

21 May 1953, Lima

Dear Tito,

I know you're right [to complain] that you only receive copies of letters written to your brother and sister, and you feel a bit neglected. It is not that I have forgotten you or for any other reason but the surcharge of work I currently have at the office. . . .

From Walter to Tito at Brooks School

5 May 1953, Lima

Dear Tito,

. . . Today in [several] magazines, especially the *U.S. News and World Report*, which I receive every week, I read about the inquiries the State Department is making at universities and colleges. It has dealt with the subject fairly broadly. It is too complex to treat in one letter, and deeds on the ground will show how government agents are carrying out these plans. One thing cannot be denied, and that is the universal danger posed by Communism for both intellectuals and non-intellectuals. We have seen that in practice it is as bad as or maybe worse than Nazism. On the other hand, it is quite natural that the State Department wants to prevent it from taking root or expanding in the universities, and it is a pity that it somehow limits the freedom of education. . . .

━━━━━━━

The letters to Helen are softer, sweeter, and kinder. She, too, was a good student and Walter teases her, saying he is surprised by her good marks.

━━━━━━━

From Walter to his daughter Helen (Neisser) Modenesi at Abbot Academy, Andover, Massachusetts [Part of a letter to all three children]

14 May 1952, Lima

Dear Helen:

I do not like your last idea, taking a boat instead of an airplane, for 3 reasons: 1. Instead of arriving in early June, you would arrive in late June; 2. Tito is staying at Harvard; and 3. Just because.

Your shopping list is accepted, but remember that when you arrive it will be winter here and autumn upon your return to the United States. So you must be careful what you buy. The things you no longer need in the U.S.A. you can send home and declare them to be:

USED   PERSONAL   EFFECTS—UNACCOMPANIED BAGGAGE

━━━━━━━

Since Rudy, the rebellious son, requests, begs, and wants, Walter advises, cajoles, and sometimes threatens. Walter's first letter to Rudy, dated May 1947, was written while Walter was on a Rotarian work-holiday trip to the US, and the last letter was dated December 1958, less than two years before his death. Although Walter recognized himself in Rudy, he shows little patience with him, mostly because he did not understand Rudy's learning disability. He exhorts him to study and apply himself, for he cannot accept mediocrity in anyone, much less in his own children. He reproaches Rudy for not listening, then assures him that once he is in his twenties, he will find his way.

After several years and a change to an alternative school, the Happy Valley School in Ojai, California, Walter uses sarcasm and tells Rudy that if he wants to become a sculptor, he should make busts of his siblings. At one point Walter threatens that unless Rudy studies, he will take only the two other children to Mexico and Guatemala. Walter rails at Rudy's desire to come back to Lima to finish school, then changes his mind and gives his permission. Of course, once he is allowed to return, Rudy chooses to stay in the US. If Rudy doesn't finish high school, Walter threatens, he could become eligible for the Peruvian draft and find himself spending two years in the military. Walter can run his many business responsibilities, his innumerable welfare association responsibilities, and his hobbies, but he cannot manage Rudy.

━━━━━━━━━

From Walter to his son Juan Rodolfo (Rudy) at Brooks School, North Andover, Massachusetts

Early January 1949, Lima

My dear Rudy!

I'm still very busy . . . In a few days I'll take some time to write in detail. Did you see the report that they sent me in December? You're too noisy and don't put enough effort into your work. I would like you to start working more conscientiously and lay the foundations to become a good architect someday.

Affectionately, Papi

From Walter to Rudy

17 January 1949, Lima

My dear Rudy!

The photos I received by regular mail are pretty good. Thank you very much! Mami wrote me you are going to photograph the teachers and I hope those will be even better. I would like you to send me small prints of them. The movies I've made with the new movie camera are of much better quality than those I took before with the Kodak. [They are] much crisper, with well-drawn contrasts. On my birthday, more than 60 people saw them, and I also recognized Philipp in the film. Are you still in contact with [him?]? You have never written me about the visits you made to his family and the families of other friends. I really want to know about their families and their homes and your impressions. Maybe you can write me about them, even if it is later. . . . There is a water scarcity in the highlands and in Lima it is rainy and cold. Today is Eva's birthday. She is still very cute and super nice. I will go to congratulate her.

Much love. Papi

From Walter to Rudy

19 January 1949, Lima

My dear Rudy,

We have had our Rotary lunch, now at the Union Club facing our main office, and I had the opportunity to chat with Dr. Wagner, who had just received a letter from you. He was very surprised [to hear] that you had grown so accustomed to Colegio San Andrés that you wanted to return to the school. He says that while you were there, you were constantly complaining . . . saying that the director was a donkey, the teachers useless and stupid, and the only star was: Rodolfo Neisser. In addition, the Champagnat School was much superior and all of Rudy Neisser's friends were there. I now remember all those conversations very well, so finally where do we stand?? The result is that you're right and I'm the fool. The Brooks School costs me more than $2,000 [US] a year for you, and here the school costs me only $40 per; consequently I have spoken with the director of San Andrés and you can go back to your old school again on June 9. I think you can bear 3 more months of study in the U.S.A. I'm sorry I already paid the Brooks School until June 4 because there will be classes only in February and March. In April there are vacations again and then one more month of school until June 3. . . .

From Walter to Rudy

Late November 1949, Lima

My dear Rudy,

I sincerely regret you did not much like my last letter that refers to your visit to Peru . . . So I beg you that in the future you no longer write me about the teacher's injustice or that he was bad or that

<u>he</u> was good for nothing. Get used to being <u>honest</u> with yourself and others and learn to recognize the <u>good</u> of others, and if so, the bad in yourself. No human being is perfect, and like you, [everyone] has good characteristics and foibles. The teacher also has them, but you'll forgive me if I cannot admit that it is <u>always</u> the other's fault and <u>never</u> your own. If I did not have a very good opinion of your intentions and principles, I would not write this, but I have a very bad opinion of your philosophy and your basic knowledge, and yes, you do not take your obligation to study seriously enough. I'm sorry I have to deal with this problem so seriously but I see that you have not yet learned to judge yourself and [instead] judge others. I want to help and am not just writing words but expressing my way of feeling and thinking.

I know it is customary for the younger generation to consider antiquated the ideas of the older generation, their commercial morality and their fair treatment of the old. Perhaps you are right. Girlfriends, the new era of television and airplanes, and the atomic bomb have brought a certain contempt to such virtues as courtesy, discipline, keeping promises, paying your debts, and doing a little more than is demanded. But I do not accept this and I know many, many others who don't accept it either. I do not want you to think I am "old fashioned" or old, nor do I want you to be honest, punctual, reliable and studious <u>for me</u>. I want you to be all this for your own good and to take advantage of your college training so it will be deeply etched in your mind and in your heart and provide a solid and healthy base for your whole life. I do not think that during your lifetime the world will be completely irresponsible and inconsiderate. Nor do I believe that the apparent lack of moral behavior among today's younger generation will be appropriate or preferred; [but instead the behavior of those who] practice a healthy and stable [lifestyle] and who are respectful, strict, punctual and honest. And so, being a father, I am too close to you; take this advice seriously, I beg you; just look around you carefully and see which qualities and human characters have reached the highest success in the country where you currently live. Put more effort and greater understanding into your work and you'll see that luck will also accompany you. But luck alone, without effort, does not exist.

Love and hugs, your Papi

From Walter to Rudy

11 January 1950, Lima

My dear Rudy

. . . Surely you've noticed that you have been in the U.S.A. for over a year, but apparently you have not realized you are there to prepare yourself for a career and for life. First you say you want to be an engineer, then a singer, a painter and today a composer. Naturally all are very acceptable and honorable professions and in all of them you can achieve something, but always only with the necessary preparation. In your last letter you say you want to become a composer and write, "Even though, I'm sure, you won't like it." Your mistake! I do not know why I should not like that my son Rudy be a great composer . . . . the mediocre, in any profession, don't get very far . . . .

From Walter to Rudy

14 May 1952 [Part of a letter to all three children]

Dear Rudy:

We received your two letters, and after long reflection, we plead guilty. Guilty because I recognize that according to the laws of genetics, you have inherited everything that is bad from both me and your mother.

I recognize that you are governed by different rules and formalities than others. Guilty because you were born Jewish, but I'm afraid you confuse religion with religiosity. Having a religion is one thing and being religious is another. Now if you protest, [remember] I have never tried to change your character because character depends on many factors and time; having different ideas and opinions is natural; if we all had the same ideas the world would be very boring.

I accept that you are an extravagant idealist (although I'm not exactly sure what this means). My opinion is that as an intelligent being, which you are, you must also use your skills in an intelligent way.

I am also not guilty that the Peruvian government has a compulsory military service law, and we can talk about this issue once you are back in Lima.

I carry the burden of guilt for the fact that Mrs. Rajagopal will not let you attend the concert because you did something that she did not like. I don't know what you did and I regret it . . .

Hugs and greetings, Papi

———————

Although Walter states that his children should make their own choices, it is clear that he made the decisions. School holidays were a case in point. Because of the enormous distance between Peru and the United States, the children spent only their long school holidays, June to August, in Lima. Arrangements had to be made for every Thanksgiving, Christmas, and spring break.

From Walter to Rudy

5 December 1949, Lima

My dear Rudy,

Many thanks for your lines on the 30/11/49 which I received today and am answering immediately. First, I'm glad that you consult me about your holidays, although generally you are fairly free to decide what to do. But often it is advisable to consult, and I advise that you do so in most cases, because four eyes see more than two. For example, in the case of Jose's invitation, I think the family will be in NY too short a time, and their funds, in dollars, are scarce, which naturally one cannot say, to make the holiday in that very expensive city very pleasant. You would not see or hear a lot; whereas my friend Art Jumper is a lot better off, has children your age, and in my opinion, would offer much more than Jose. [You'll] have enough time to chat during spring break. In addition, I have already accepted the invitation at Mr. Jumper's on your behalf and I would be pleased if you would now accept and thank him. I am quite sure you will have a lovely holiday and you should get to know the country and its people. Helen had also been invited to two places and also has to go to the place agreed to beforehand since I believe it to be more convenient. I have not yet received the grades and I'm glad you've improved. Say hello to Tito and a hug for you

from your Papi

In his letters to his children, Walter writes about the family but conveys mostly good news. We do not have a single letter where deaths are mentioned, and since we have almost all of Walter's letters to Rudy, I have to conclude that bad news was conveyed in person. During the period Walter's children were away, Martha, Fanny, and most of the members of the older generation died, leaving only Tante Regina and Onkel Josef. I was not allowed to attend my grandmother Martha's funeral even though I was fourteen years old. I was told about other deaths only upon my return from university in the US. Children were "spared."

Regina Nothmann and Josef Nothmann at the Jewish old people's home, Afilantis, the brainchild of Curt Nothmann. 1961.

In 1951, Walter took his immediate family on a grand three-month tour of Europe. This is the first mention of it to the children, from their mother.

From Erna (Lustig) Neisser to her son Rudy and her daughter Helen at school in Massachusetts

10 April 1951, Lima

My dear Helen and Rudy,

What joy I had on Monday when your letters arrived. I see that you had nice holidays and now are going to start the last school semester with new vigor before heading into the summer holidays. These two months will fly by and Papi has finally decided we will go to Europe. He is going to buy a large, comfortable car in advance and send it to Portugal, where we will begin our excursion; we'll visit friends, the Ballesters, then Seville, Madrid, southern France, Switzerland and Italy. For years it has been Papi's ideal to travel with his children, who are now old enough to enjoy the beauties of the old continent. Now Papi is working hard. Tomorrow he is going to Trujillo and Chiclayo and I hope to have him back for the week-end. . . . Well, my dear chicks, we will see each other soon, behave yourselves, study hard and I send you all my affection.

Your, Mami

From Walter to Helen

4 May 1951, Lima

Young lady,

. . . I have now more or less prepared the itinerary for the trip we will take and this program constitutes my idea in accordance with all of your wishes and can be corrected, increased or decreased depending on the circumstances.

We will leave New York on the *Western Dann*, a steamer of the Royal Netherland Steamship Co., on June 16. We arrive in Rotterdam on June 21. We stay in Holland a few days and continue to Paris to pick up the large Citroen. Unfortunately it cannot be the Silver Jaguar Tito wanted because it is not large enough for us, nor [can it be] a convertible, since we have to put the bags on the roof. From there we continue to Spain, then Switzerland and Italy. We will go via Switzerland or Austria to Germany, and after that to Denmark, Sweden, Norway, and England. On August 25 we embark again and will be back in New York on September 3rd.

Since we are 5 persons, we will have to pack carefully. We will need special clothes for the ship, and then only whatever is necessary to carry in the car. We have to take only flat suitcases plus two hand bags for small things that can be tucked out of the way during the trip.

I wonder what clothes and dresses you plan to take. For the car you will need a skirt and blouse or a light suit, a tailored suit for teas, dances, etc., an outfit for daily use, and the appropriate underwear.

From Walter to Rudy

21 May 1951

. . . In New York, Mami will get the visas we need for the different countries we will visit; and for this purpose, you need to send 12 passport pictures as well as your passport to H. John Northman, 11 E. 57th Street, <u>Certified post</u>. To that end, it would be best if you would take the pictures in a "photo booth" or another inexpensive way. I have not yet received the list of things you want to bring along on the trip. I will bring 2 pairs of English gabardine pants that I have had made to measure here, so they will last.

[Handwritten] I await your prompt news and am sending, attached, a letter from Ruth. All others will send you many greetings and some have written. Best wishes for your day [his birthday, May 27] and a big hug from

your Papi

From Walter to Rudy

2 June 1951, Lima

Thanks to Tito's foresight, for he wrote me that you might all have difficulty returning to the United States from Europe, I have immediately contacted the American Embassy here, and they tell me that you need a record from your school that you plan to enroll in the next school year, plus a good-conduct police certificate. They suggest that each one of you get a re-entry permit.

━━━━━━━

That year Walter was fifty-four, at the height of his success; Erna fifty-three, elegant and pleased with her world; Tito, Rudy, and Helen were nineteen, eighteen, and seventeen years old, teenagers who, by their looks in the picture opposite, desperately wanted to be somewhere else. In the end, rather than buy a Citroen, Walter had a large green Oldsmobile shipped to Europe, and for three months they took in all the Western European sights between Scandinavia and Portugal. Although Walter and Erna had planned this as a cultural experience, Rudy's most striking recollection is that they all learned how to drive well, and that Walter shipped the Olds back to Lima, where many admired it for years.

Back in Lima, the rest of the family, unable to travel because they were both stateless and far poorer, followed the European tour with great interest. And they loved the movies Walter had taken. Walter, in turn, prepared carefully for family movie evenings. He took a postcard of the Brussels Mannekin Pis, the iconic sculpture of a naked boy urinating into a fountain, replaced the boy's face

Walter, Erna, Rudy, Helen, and Tito on the family trip to Europe. 1951.

with Rudy's, and filmed the postcard. The image appeared on the screen to great laughter.

Walter's version of the Mannekin Pis.   *The real Mannekin Pis in Brussels.*

In a letter to Helen he alludes to perhaps one of the most difficult problems, the rift with his beloved cousin Curt Nothmann. Walter's mother, Martha, and Curt's father, Moritz, were siblings, and like Walter, Curt had lost his older brother in the First World

War, which may have fostered a strong bond between them. Curt was among the very first to come to Peru. Working with Walter since 1935, he had become one of his closest business associates. But in 1951 he quit and formed a company that competed directly with Neisser and Co. Not only did he leave with more than fifteen years of knowledge on running the business, but he also took along several key employees. The rift split the family, some taking Walter's side, others Curt's, and cousins stopped talking to each other.

━━━━━━━━━

From Walter to Helen

2 April 1952, Lima [Letter mostly in German.]
. . . Here in the office I have a lot to do at the moment, because (1) Mr. Herzka [Walter's second-in-command] has gone to the States on vacation with his whole family for two months. He will telephone Tito to see if you can meet with him. (2) As you know, we are on war footing with Curt Nothmann. He has opened a business just like Neisser and Co., organized in the same form, and is trying in any way, unfortunately in a very dirty fashion, to compete [with us]. Last month he hired away Engineer Larrabure, head of the installations department, and now I must necessarily become head of installations and reorganize the whole department. This of course makes for a lot of work and takes my time away from other tasks, so for example, yesterday evening I had to stay in the office until 9 p.m. As you can understand, this is no fun for me but unfortunately it can't be changed. Curt Nothmann [switches mid-sentence to Spanish] has ugly ways to compete, but competition is always good for business [back to German] if you are strong

and don't let yourself go. Now I spend some office hours in my own office, others in the installation department, and the rest in Herzka's department. In addition, my new secretary had to leave because she has very bad eyes and has to get them in order . . . Therefore it is unfortunately not possible for me to write many private letters, since I have to sit myself in front of the typewriter and it takes away time that I need for other things. . . . Otherwise here all are healthy and well, and Nélida Odnopossoff, the sister of the violinist and the viola player, is staying with us for the next 10 days, and she'll give several piano concerts.

━━━━━━━━

The business quarrel between Walter and Curt spilled over to family matters, specifically the inheritance of their Tante Bianka—sister of Walter's mother and Curt's father—who had married very well and had led an affluent life in Berlin. In April 1937 Bianka joined her family, who had earlier moved to Amsterdam. Records from Camp Westerbork, a Nazi detention and transit camp that assembled Jews and Romani in Holland, show that six years later, in April 1943, she was confined for six weeks, then released. Her son, a member of the Jewish Council, the conduit the Nazis used to convey their commands, had been able to protect her. Nevertheless, by August of the same year, her son, his first wife, his second wife, her grandson, and Bianka were interned at Camp Westerbork. Then, between January and September 1944, they were all deported to Theresienstadt. One month later her son, one daughter-in-law, and her grandson were transported to Auschwitz. Her son and grandson were killed on October 1 and her daughter-in-law on October 11, 1944. When Bianka made contact with the family after the war, her two nephews,

Walter Neisser and Curt Nothmann, facilitated her trip to Peru and in May 1946 set her up in a tiny house within walking distance of her brothers and sister. She was a broken woman, very different from the others in the family. She died in 1955, nine years after arriving in Lima.

But Bianka's story was far from over. In the early 1950s the German authorities began making restitutions, the so-called *Wiedergutmachung* ("to make good again"), paying German marks in reparation for the sins of the Nazis. They calculated the amount of the restitution according to the suffering and loss. Bianka had not only lost her son, grandson, and daughter-in-law but also spent time in two concentration camps and owned some prime Berlin real estate. Bianka's wealth became a family legend and we joked about our "inheritance."

Bianka died when her restitution had been approved but not paid out, so both Walter and Curt hired lawyers to claim it. Both rightly argued they had helped her financially, brought her to Peru, and maintained her in Lima, but each suggested that he had carried the bulk of the cost. The case, lucrative for the lawyers, was settled only in the early 1970s, more than fifteen years after Bianka's death, well after one litigant, Walter, had gone to his grave. The long list of inheritors in the Neisser and Nothmann families, perhaps some forty or fifty people, received around $1,000 each, nothing short of miraculous. With my share, I bought a desk and my first electric typewriter.

In addition to monetary restitutions, in 1953 the German government offered German citizenship to those who had been stripped of it in 1941. In the early fifties, only Walter and his wife were Peruvian citizens, having been naturalized in the thirties. All the other members of our family born in Europe were stateless because the Peruvian government was unwilling to facilitate naturalization. Both Walter and my father, Erich, took the high road, saying that after the events of the Second World War they could not possibly become German citizens again. Kleine Erna, Kaethe, Ruth, and their respective husbands disagreed, arguing that they no longer wanted to be "apátridas"—stateless. They could no longer stand the instability; they needed a firm legal status. The question of accepting or refusing German citizenship led to angry arguments among the Neisser siblings and Nothmann cousins and finally to separate decisions. Most members of our family accepted; therefore my cousins and their children have German citizenship and some live and work in Europe. In the end Walter and Erich and their spouses were the only ones who refused. My parents then actively sought Peruvian citizenship, which was finally granted in 1957. My mother had worked as a nanny when she first arrived in Peru, and one of her former charges intervened on their behalf. For once an important event occurred without Walter's help.

Walter became ill in 1953 when he was fifty-six years old. He sought medical help in Boston, where he was diagnosed with leukemia. His doctor, whom he saw for extended periods of time over the next seven years, was the preeminent American clinical hematologist William Dameshek, who is credited with the first uses of chemotherapy. Walter must have developed an intimate relationship with his doctor, for in his letters he refers to him as "Onkel Doktor," and Dr. Dameshek's obituary mentions the pre-Columbian statuettes in his collection, an example of Walter's generosity.

From Walter to Rudy

9 March 1954, Lima

I'll have to travel [to Boston] the first days of May, unless the white blood cells increase more than they should, and naturally I will have to spend some time in Boston . . . . Of course this also depends on the Onkel Doktor . . . .

In his letters, Walter mentions he is trying to work fewer hours, but it is apparent that he is still at the office most of the time. He has bought land next to his country house in Santa Inés and is working to integrate the two properties.

From Walter to his children

9 July 1955, Santa Inés

My dear ones:

Chaclacayo and the hills in front of the house are still covered with mist. It is colder than normal and the sun did not rise until 8 a.m.

I have worked for three hours on the path that goes up the hill of the new property, so it looks halfway like the old one. In the middle of the new field there will be a waterfall with fish, no trees, just creepers, and I hope to leave it looking rustic.

The last few weeks I have taken advantage of my own long weekends, leaving at noon on Friday and returning to the office on Monday afternoon. Unfortunately I have not been able to reduce my workload as I had planned, for Uncle Erich had a heart attack, and because his is a "one-man-business," I've had to supervise and take responsibility for his stationery business. Luckily I am not the president of any of the Jewish organizations, nor the Pro Students League, and in July I will end my duties as Vice President of the Rotary Club. So at least in the evenings I am freer, although during the day everyone still bothers me a great deal. The worst problem is that everyone wants to talk to the boss personally, and each time I face another visitor, I have to switch the manner, the form, and the aspect of the conversation, and this is more tiring than working continuously.

In addition, we have to prepare to face new competition from Sears Roebuck since they are opening September 15, and only a few days ago our company completed the construction of a large exhibit hall and a large warehouse on Progreso St. [now called Venezuela Avenue]. The new building in Miraflores on Larco Avenue is almost ready, and we hope to have the store inauguration on August 15. I am there daily, in the mornings.

. . . As soon as they complete the new road, with one lane going up and the second coming down, I'll move to Santa Inés. The only problem is how to find bridge games, movies, concerts and other entertainment for Mami. We need a driver. . . .

The vine-covered walkway that led up to the country house in Santa Inés. Photo by Ricardo Grau.

Meanwhile Neisser and Co., like many big companies with a strong CEO, suffered from Walter's absence. Although nobody was willing to admit it, the company was not doing as well and lost its electrical monopoly with the state. Once it was clear how sick Walter was, problems arose among the company's top management. Franz Herzka, second in command, was unfairly forced out, and members of the Camet family, who had been part of the Neisser team for many years, attempted to take over. Competition continued to increase as international companies built plants and opened very large stores. Sears Roebuck not only sold appliances but also manufactured them in Peru, reducing costs considerably. The equivalent appliances sold by Neisser and Co. were all imported. Other employees learned how parts of the operation worked and left to open their own businesses. José Feliu, a Spaniard hired by Walter because of his expertise in iron and knowledge of lamp making, opened his own store only five blocks away. Other competitors at both the retail and the manufacturing level cut into profits, and an attempt to build boats for the fish-meal industry had to be scrapped, the boat design a failure.

Walter's photo of the Chimbote harbor, capital of the Peruvian fish-meal industry.

Nevertheless, Walter continued to be a shrewd businessman. In 1955, he built the new building he mentions in his letter of July 9: a seven-story building on Larco Avenue in Miraflores. His store was at street level; stories two to six had three apartments and two offices each; and the seventh floor was reserved for the domestic employees, with small rooms and a communal bathroom. Today, after several transformations and much remodeling, the building remains in the hands of Walter's children. Its location in the heart of Lima's new downtown is a testament to his foresight. Helen writes:

> My brothers and I were educated in the U.S. and it was taken for granted that when [Tito and Rudy] graduated they would work with my father. That is what Tito did after graduating from Harvard in economics (his dream was to be a teacher, but to please my father, he studied economics). Rudy, always the rebellious one, stayed in the U.S. and worked at different jobs . . . . When he returned to Lima, he also worked [for about two years] at Neisser. [My husband] Pipo also worked at Neisser, but not for a long time.

The Neisser building on Larco Avenue in Miraflores. The addition to the building at the far right, shown here during the construction period, was built after Walter's death with the proceeds from the sale of his stamp collections.

Walter in 1958.

From Walter to Helen and her husband Fernando (Pipo) Modenesi

28 November 1958, Buenos Aires, Hotel Claridge

My dear Helen and Pipo,

From the mirror the pictures of [my grandchildren] Mariana and Gaby look at me. The 3 photos that Rudy took are there and when I fix my tie and comb my hair or pass by, the pictures remind me that I should be in Santa Inés with them. I miss them and I need them. I would like to shorten the trip. Send me a picture of Roxana so I can have a complete set . . . .

And how are you, Helenutschka? Fully recovered? And you, Pipo? . . .

The trip—without a fixed itinerary—goes well. Sunday we go to Mar del Plata for 3 days at then back to Buenos Aires for 2 or 3 days, then to Bariloche. There we will rest for a month and return to Lima via Chile.

Mami shops every day—so far with little success—one has to get the lay of the land, compare prices and qualities, and so in the morning [she bought] 1 pair of shoes, another in the afternoon. 2 swimsuits—very cheap—and back in Lima she will realize what she missed.

But we are in good health and good humor. We have seen many friends and look forward to hearing from you when we get to the Tunquelén Hotel in Bariloche. Meanwhile greetings, love and hugs

from Mami and Papi

Walter, Erna, and Helen with granddaughters Mariana and Gabriela. 1958.

From Walter to Tito, Rudy, and Pipo in Lima

22 December 1958, Tunquelén, Argentina

My dear Tito, Rudy, and Pipo,

Friday morning we rented a motorboat. . . . Mami told the owner that we did not know how to fish and that he should teach us. . . . In the afternoon a boy took us out on a lake for two hours. . . . It was quite turbulent. . . . I showed her what to do so the fish would bite. Since we had to be back at the hotel by 9 p.m. we had little time, but still I caught a 9-pound salmon and another of 4 or 5 pounds. Wasn't that lucky?

But it is almost always like that in life; we have to pay a great deal of attention and luck will help us be successful. And I like strawberries with cream! But can I use strawberries instead of a fishing line or a fly to hook my fish? No! I have to place what the fish will want to grab and not what I like.

From the office, I have brought with me the little notebook where I have made daily notes of visits, meetings, conferences, etc. I have read and reread several of the discussions I have had during the present year and I have noted that many times I did not think about what the other person wanted, but only about what I wanted, and this is a big mistake. If I want my newspaper ad to have the desired effect, I have to create in the buyer, or better said, in the reader of the ad, the <u>desire</u> to buy what I am offering, and if I want the other person to do what I want, I must proceed as if I were fishing and not like the Mr. Organizer, condemning and criticizing. When my children started to smoke, I did not challenge and criticize them, but I had them see that in order to be good swimmers, they could not smoke, and so they quit [smoking]. Generally, criticizing is the worst thing we can do because criticism automatically <u>obliges</u> the other person to take a defensive position, and now, by reading these daily notes, I notice that in the future I have to read them weekly, instead of at the end of the year, in order to avoid so many mistakes and to improve my performance. By reading them again and doing a self-criticism, one learns a lot. We have to eliminate the criticism of our system, and instead of condemning, show appreciation and praise. When having a discussion with a person, we have to try to understand the other person's point of view and not only our own and I'm sure we'll profit a lot. Perhaps you also could adopt this policy <u>immediately</u> and my notes during the next year will be <u>very different</u> from those I have had to make about our different discussions in this year that is about to end. They have been criticism, criticism, criticism.

Henry Ford said, "If there is any one secret of success, it lies in the ability to get the other person's point of view and see things from his angle as well as from your own."

Let's try to imitate him and may the success he has had accompany you. Keep smiling, don't criticize and try to make other person wish to do what <u>you want</u> him to do.

Also, may 1959 be a year of health and success.

Affectionately, Papi

═══════════

Walter died in 1960, and without him at its head, Neisser and Co. did not survive. It had already begun its decline in the previous decade, but it floundered in his absence. He had been the founder, had had the foresight to predict the good times and the bad. The times were not propitious, the government in power unfriendly to business, competition was fierce, Neisser was no longer the sole provider of electricity, and the company failed. Helen writes, "It was a pity since it was a prestigious and successful chain of stores for over 30 years."

For the Neisser and Nothmann families, the Peruvian years were almost over. We were part of a trend that saw the Peruvian

Jewish community shrink from 5,500 in the 1960s to 2,200 in the new millennium. The creation of the state of Israel had a profound effect on the community. In 1947, thanks to his many government contacts, Walter played an important role in convincing Peruvian politicians to vote in favor of the creation of the new state. His name was put forward as the potential Honorary Israeli Consul but he was adamant in refusing any public office. Walter's three children, who had left Peru in 1948 and lived in their boarding school cocoons, were immune to the shift in the community. But Walter, quite typically, was one of the first to visit the newly-founded state, and many members of the community saw Israel as the next step in their life journey. They had fled Nazi persecution in Europe and arrived in Peru a mere ten years earlier, but they had not integrated into Peruvian society. This was the case not only for those born in Europe but also for their Peruvian-born children. Several Zionist groups recruited actively with great success. Many left. In percentage terms, the Peruvian contingent was the largest from South America. Our family was quite typical, with two young people making aliyah. Kleine Erna's son Miguel / Michael and Guenter Nothmann's son Frank left for Israel, although both later moved to North America.

Walter, Erna, Walter's brother and sisters, the many aunts, uncles, and cousins are all buried in the Jewish cemetery in Lima. Of his generation, Curt and his wife Tilde Nothmann as well as Thea Nothmann moved back to Germany. The next generation dispersed, leaving only Walter's three children, their families, and a handful of others in Peru. Most of us now live in the United States, Canada, and several Latin American capitals, others in Europe and Israel. Some are practicing Jews, others consider themselves cultural

Jews, and still others are no longer Jewish. But all of us are convinced that had it not been for Walter, we would not be here today to tell his, and our, story.

Although we have many letters, Walter never mentioned his philanthropy, and it was only through the beneficiaries or third parties that we obtained this information. In one letter to Rudy he goes on at length about the comparative costs of education in the United States and Peru, but does not mention that in Lima he is busy giving out scholarships. The Rotary Club's Wenceslao F. Molina Foundation gave university students of scant means loans to buy textbooks and specialized equipment. After his father's death a chance acquaintance told Rudy that Walter had paid both his high school and university tuition, the only proviso being that he come to the office on Mantas Street and personally show Walter his grades. In addition we heard about Johnny Wertheimer, a local teenager who suffered disfiguring burns in a car race. Walter paid his very sizable hospital and rehabilitation bills and provided limitless support. Walter's granddaughter Roxana Modenesi Neisser, born two years before his death, recounts the following experience:

> I walked into a car dealership in Miami along with my ex-husband and his brother to buy a car to ship to Peru. The offices were behind an opaque glass window and after a few minutes an elderly man came out and addressed me in German, certain that I would understand. "Du bist Neisser," he said, and I responded "Ja." His eyes watered and he said I looked like my grandfather, same eyes, same hair. He told me that because of Walter he had been able to leave Germany and take his family

to Peru, to make a life there, to have grandchildren. He added that his family would never forget the person who had allowed them to live. . . . Only then, after this episode, did I understand my grandfather's importance in the lives of so many people and I feel proud to have his name.

Acknowledgments

MY thanks go first to my cousins Helen (Neisser) Modenesi, Rudy Neisser, and Tito's widow, Edith (Frankfurter) Neisser, who kept letters, photographs, and all manner of realia. Helen helped the most. At the very beginning she scanned and made letters and pictures into twenty-first-century tools; then, for several years, she patiently answered my innumerable questions and read and proofed and corrected until the manuscript was complete. We have communicated constantly, often several times a day, over a four-year period.

In addition, I would like to thank all the members of the extended Nothmann and Neisser families, especially Ronny Angress and Frank Nothmann. Frank sent his grandmother's entire correspondence and the letters, pictures, and cards related to his uncle John (Hans) Nothmann's concentration camp experience. He and Ronny Angress answered questions without end. Ronny was a fount of information. Lutz Berger wrote that he had been on the Kindertransport to England and made this part of our story even more poignant. The other relatives who helped are too numerous to list but I would like to make special mention of some I met only because of this project: Mark Neisser and his sister Carol Welsh,

Patricia Neisser, Gerardo Espinosa, and Helen's cousin, Roger Lustig. Other cousins added details and made corrections.

While I worked on the letters, three of my first cousins died: Kaethe's daughters Ursula and Vera Simenauer and Kleine Erna's son Miguel / Michael Liebermann. Miguel's genealogical trees of our various families were invaluable throughout the project.

In theory the letters and pictures were the skeleton of our story and all I had to do was add some flesh, but when the scans were first in my hands, I—who had volunteered to do something with our family story—balked and proclaimed the task too difficult. Because Helen and Rudy no longer read much German, the pages from the letters were out of order, and those from a letter by one relative were followed by pages from quite another. In many cases the people who had penned the letters were long dead and I had no points of reference. Armed with many years of teaching and marking papers before the computer age, I began by matching the handwriting.

The original texts are written in German, although there are also letters in Spanish and even a few in English. Some of the German letters have words and sometimes entire paragraphs in another language. The German letters are written in two scripts: Sütterlin, used only between 1915 and 1941, which posed the greatest difficulty; and modern German. In Sütterlin a single letter has many written variations depending on whether it is at the beginning, middle, or end of a word and if it is capitalized or lower case. I would never have completed this project without the assistance of Petra Zangerl, the late Hans Kaal, Christine Mayr, and especially Sabine Meyr, who helped me decipher the Sütterlin script. In most cases my helpers read the letters aloud and I furiously recorded them in longhand. It was painstaking work, and one letter could take several sessions. There were always gaps related to either the script or the condition of the original. Sabine Meyr went through all the documents like a detective, figured out missing words, and made corrections. Of course some of the correspondence was much easier. The letters written in the 1940s are in modern script and there are many typewritten letters.

There were many surprises. I had no idea that Walter had spent time in both Argentina and Chile before coming to Peru, and I was very impressed with his descriptions of both countries. I was flabbergasted to learn that my aunt Kleine Erna, who arrived in Peru in 1933, returned to Germany in 1935, most probably to find a husband, then left Germany for a second time. It was also astonishing to discover that even in the face of Nazi persecution, Grosse Erna's mother came to Peru very reluctantly and took many months deciding to give up her apartment and sell her furniture in Germany. But beyond anything, it was their German identity that came through overwhelmingly, from Walter's volunteering to serve as a soldier in the First World War, to his brother's grave marked as having died for the Fatherland, to their reluctance to leave Germany, and finally to continue to speak and eat and think like German Jews while living out the rest of their lives in Peru. Walter and his wife Erna were the only exceptions.

There are many people whom I would like to thank for their help, encouragement, and support. Several friends read the manuscript and made suggestions, including Elaine Kalman, Lorne Lerner, Lisi and Suzanne Gardiner, and my daughter, Margo Echenberg. Michelle Green Echenberg worked miracles on the old photographs and rendered hundred-year-old pictures usable. Tony Shine designed the family trees, and my son David Echenberg advised, modified and generally calmed fears related to the contract.

A very special thank you goes to Suzanne Gardiner, who over a period of more than thirty years insisted that Walter's story needed to be told. When it became clear that I could not bring the book to fruition, my good friend Judy Sklar Rasminsky stepped in. Without her editorial help, the final manuscript never would have taken shape. Myron, always my first reader, was as insightful and helpful as ever. I am deeply grateful to all.

Glossary

Chevra kadisha: Burial society.

Mischpoche: Family, from the Hebrew.

Ostjuden: Yiddish-speaking Jews from the East. Derogatory expression used by German Jews.

Sefer torah: "Torah scroll(s)." A handwritten copy of the Torah, the holiest book within Judaism. It must meet extremely strict standards of production. The Torah scroll is mainly used in the ritual of Torah reading during Jewish services. It contains the Five Books of Moses.

Tefillin: Also called **phylacteries.** Comprising a set of small black leather boxes containing scrolls of parchment inscribed with verses from the Torah, worn by observant Jews during weekday morning prayers.

Yekke: Derogatory expression referring to German Jews.